To

_____

From

_____

Date

_____

#Peaces Series, Volume 1

Waiting Compass
Finding God when He seems to delay

JOSEPH OLA

Copyright © 2018 Joseph Ola
All rights reserved.
ISBN: 9781729154786

Word Alive
Liverpool, UK

Bible versions used include:
Contemporary English Version (CEV) Copyright © 1995 by American Bible Society; Easy-to-Read Version (ERV) Copyright © 2006 by Bible League International; English Standard Version (ESV) The Holy Bible, English Standard Version Copyright © 2001 by Crossway Bibles, a publishing ministry of Good News Publishers.; GOD'S WORD Translation (GW) Copyright © 1995 by God's Word to the Nations. Used by permission of Baker Publishing Group; Good News Translation (GNT) Copyright © 1992 by American Bible Society; International Children's Bible (ICB) The Holy Bible, International Children's Bible® Copyright© 1986, 1988, 1999, 2015 by Tommy Nelson™, a division of Thomas Nelson. Used by permission; King James Version (KJV) Public Domain. Living Bible (TLB) The Living Bible copyright © 1971 by Tyndale House Foundation. Used by permission of Tyndale House Publishers Inc., Carol Stream, Illinois 60188. All rights reserved.; The Message (MSG) Copyright © 1993, 1994, 1995, 1996, 2000, 2001, 2002 by Eugene H. Peterson; New Century Version (NCV) The Holy Bible, New Century Version®. Copyright © 2005 by Thomas Nelson, Inc. New International Version (NIV) Holy Bible, New International Version®, NIV® Copyright ©1973, 1978, 1984, 2011 by Biblica, Inc.® Used by permission. All rights reserved worldwide.; New Living Translation (NLT) Holy Bible. New Living Translation copyright© 1996, 2004, 2007, 2013 by Tyndale House Foundation. Used by permission of Tyndale House Publishers Inc., Carol Stream, Illinois 60188. All rights reserved. The Passion Translation (TPT) The Passion Translation®. Copyright © 2017 by BroadStreet Publishing® Group, LLC. Used by permission. All rights reserved. thePassionTranslation.com

Author's Contact Address
+447752398481
www.josephkolawole.org
hello@josephkolawole.org
ng.linkedin.com/in/olakolawole
www.facebook.com/josephkolawole

To the staff and students of
Life Church College
—past, present and future.

Contents

	Acknowledgments	ix
	Series Introduction	13
	Hello, God's Hero!	17
	Preface	25
1	Track 1: God is in His Agenda	31
2	Track 2: God is in His Time	43
3	Track 3: God is in Your Trust	53
4	Track 4: God is in Your Perseverance	71
5	Track 5: God is in Your Contentment	83
	The God of Happy Endings	127
	I Will Wait For Him	137
	References	141

Acknowledgments

More than a few people deserve to be celebrated and appreciated with regards to making this book become a reality. Below, I have only mention a handful of them by name:

Gideon and Beatrice Ola, you two are parents like no other! Thanks for parenting me and my siblings in love.

Pastor Dr. G.O. Olutola (JP), your life is an inexhaustible bundle of leadership lessons. Thanks for being a father indeed. Pastor S.O. Ilesanmi, I'm proud to have found my footing in ministry under your tutelage.

Prof. and Prof. (Mrs) Fatusi, thanks for nurturing me consistently and for not giving up on me.

Olusola and Oriade, only God can repay the love you've shown to me and 'mine'. Feranmi, Nifemi and Tife are blessed to call you Dad and Mum.

Rich Martin, thanks for your liberating leadership. Pastor Tosin and Elizabeth Ogunsanlu, thanks for opening your doors to me. Pastors Dara and Abiola Shofoluwe, I couldn't have hoped for better parents in a foreign land. Pastor (Dr) and Mrs Davies, thanks for your parental care. Dr. and Mrs Tope Lawal, thanks for your relentless care and support. Femi and Tinuola Ajayi, you two are destiny helpers!

Dr and Mrs Oladapo, thanks for being my family away from family.

Samson, Paolo, John, and my awesome Life Church College colleagues and leaders, you all have made my Bradford experience memorable.

Ibukun Oyetunji, you are the best at what you do! TAC Powerline Assembly, thanks for giving me a great ministry "take-off"!

AanuOluwapo (Eleos), you are the girl that coloured my childish paintings; the lady that saturated my teenage wonderings; and the woman that *wifed* me in my heart's portrait—the one my vision sung to before the beginning began! Thanks for staying by me.

Having saved the best for last, I want to say a big "thank you" to the Prince of Peace who gave His unbroken peace to my broken pieces; holding me in #peaces, lest I fall to pieces.

WAITING COMPASS

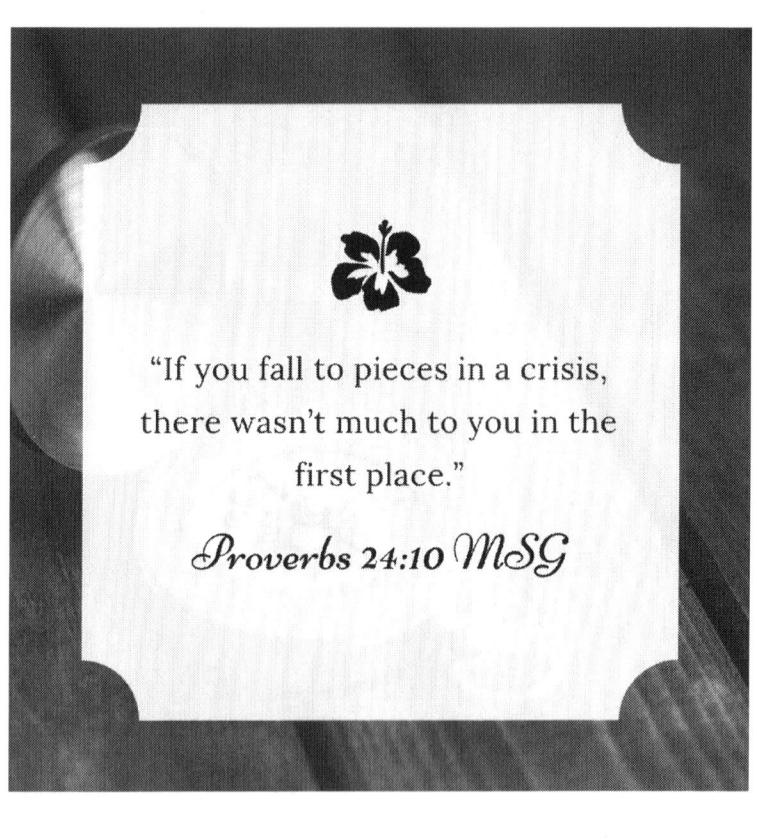

"If you fall to pieces in a crisis, there wasn't much to you in the first place."

Proverbs 24:10 MSG

Series Introduction

GOD GIVES HIS HELP IN #PEACES

Life happens. Joy and sorrow, questions and answers; life is an unending symphony of rock and blues. Be that as it may, we seem to do better with the joys and answers but shattered to pieces at the sight or earshot of sorrow and questions. Consequently, each one of us is a walking bunch of broken pieces held loosely in frame by the hopes and answers we live for—the next good news, the next joy, the next celebration.
But...
What if that next joy is delayed? What happens when pain is all we feel? What is our lot when we face

danger, or disappointment, or even death? And how do we answer life's big questions—Who am I? Where did I come from? What on earth am I here for? What can I do? Who do I marry? How can I overcome negative addictions? Where am I going when I die? Why will a good God allow evil in His world? Why am I still single, or unemployed or childless, or sick, or dying? Where is God in all of these? (And as long as our postal address is yet to end in 'New Jerusalem', these are realities and questions we will continue to live through.)

Our broken pieces of trust in God either gets further shattered and scattered as we reason out the answers to these questions or we may seek to lay hold on that which can hold our broken pieces together in times like that.

Solomon said:

> *"If you fall to pieces in a crisis, there wasn't much to you in the first place."*
> *(Proverbs 24:10 MSG)*

Here's what I've found to be true for those whose ultimate trust is in God: **God gives His help in 'peaces'.** There's a genre of peace for every situation and for every question life may throw at us. In life's delays and in disappointments; in its confusions and contentions—God's ever-present help is given in 'peaces'.

This series (#Peaces) was written to offer such 'Peaces' of God's help which we can hold on to so that when the unpleasant realities of life becomes our circumstance or when life throws at us questions beyond the scope of our finite mind, we will be held in #peaces, lest we fall to pieces.

The first instalment in this series explores the subject of God's delays.

Let's dig in.

Joseph Kolawole Ola
www.josephkolawole.org

Hello, God's Hero!

The other day, Lydia demanded to speak with me. She's a good friend and a junior colleague back in my first degree days at Obafemi Awolowo University, Nigeria. She's a respectable young lady and a committed disciple of Jesus. Looking for an exemplary 'lady of virtue'? She's the real deal. Sharp mind. Beautiful face. Godly heart. Lydia had it all together.

So you can understand my emotional reaction when she started talking. (I'll leave the emotional reaction bit to later.) She took me through a journey of her life's story. Things she's been praying for since she was a teenager that are yet to happen—or even worse, that happened exactly in the opposite of her request. Despite her undeniable brilliance, she finished her first degree with a 2-2 (and she had an extra year). Her present job and her intended career path don't look alike. Her mates are hosting their second baby shower—she's yet to be married.

Of course, compared to the story of someone else in your world—or even yours—Lydia's story might seem trivial, but at the end of the day, pain and disappointments are relative. They highlight a common element, though. There are those moments when life just seems to reprogram our thinking with a configuration of doubt in the faithfulness of the God that claims to love us and Who we claim to love. You start questioning your sincerity.

> *Is there something you are not doing right? Is there deception beneath your actions? Is there—truly—a God that cares? If He does care, then what's up? Why am I here? Why are my mates gone so far ahead and everything just seem to be dragging on my side of the world and unpleasant family cycles seem to be repeating itself in my life? God, are you there???*

That was her question.

I guess it may sound okay if 'some other people' ask that kind of question—but Lydia? She broke down in tears on the phone. She's fed up.

And then came my emotional reaction. I swallowed a lump. Then another. Then my voice went shaky, and the next minute I was sniffling to mute my tears. Initially, I thought I won't say anything to her. I felt all that God would have me say to her is a few words:

> *"Baby girl, as clearly as I can hear you on the other end of the line, God is hearing you. Only infinitely more!"*

That's all I thought I would say. But the more I opened my mouth, the more my own suppression of my 'disappointment in God' found expression. A couple of weeks earlier, my wife and I dedicated our son in the church — four days to our first wedding anniversary. As good an experience as that was, my pastoral heart processed the experience as mixed feelings. In the same congregation where I'm privileged to serve in a pastoral capacity, there are couples who had been married for much longer than my wife and I and are still 'waiting on God' for the 'fruit of the womb'. There are a couple of other couples that I've met in my pastoral journey in Nigeria who are in the same shoes and we are still praying the same prayers we've prayed for years concerning them. Deep in my heart, I felt like it's not fair.

But how do you communicate that, pastorally?

As Lydia and I kept talking, a song started playing in the background of my heart. (That's not the first time God will bring me a song when I'm processing clashing thoughts with a counselee.) It was Amanda Cook's song—HEROES. That was a song I listened to repeatedly at a season of my life while in Bible College. God, I believe, highlighted a line for me to mention in my conversation with Lydia. The line says:

> *"You have taught my feet to dance upon disappointments, and I will worship you."*

Seriously? What kind of loving God does that? What kind of loving God teaches you a choreography that will be stunning only on the stage of disappointments?

While I was still processing that with Lydia, God reminded me of the message I preached in church two Sundays before this conversation. In my congregation, for that month, we explored the theme of 'Divine Acceleration'. We were persuaded that God gave us that phrase for that month, and so we *prayed* and *declared* and *claimed* and did everything thinkable with that theme, unwavering in our hope that God will (begin to) hasten to perform His promises over our lives. But on that Sunday, the message God gave me for the congregation (as we wrapped up the series) was titled: "WAITING: The Fast Track to Divine Acceleration."

I know what you are thinking: *Does that even make sense?* That the quick way to partake of the blessing of divine acceleration is to…what? To *wait*? Of course, it doesn't make sense. But look through the scriptures and you'll find out that the testimonies of divine acceleration that you find have been preluded by a season of waiting—sometimes for years!

Examples? Joseph. He became a prime minister in one day—without an electoral process or candidate screening. He didn't need to bring proof of his education or birth certificate. He was not a card-carrying member of Pharaoh's Dictatorial Party, in fact, he was not an Egyptian. Yet, overnight, he switched from being a prisoner to becoming a prime minister. Don't be deceived, the two statuses might begin with the same alphabet, but that's as far as they are similar. Last night, he slept in a dungeon, tonight, he's sleeping in the Prime Minister's Villa. In reality, however, he's had to wait for 2 hours in a dry well. 2 months on the road from Dothan to Egypt. Only God knows how long he stayed on the 'slaves market' before Potiphar bought him. Bible scholars believe he spent a decade in Potiphar's house—waiting for his teenage dream to come to pass. Add to that about another year in the prison before he met the king's cupbearer whose dream he interpreted. And then another 2 full years (24 months!) before the cupbearer remembered to mention to the king that there's a 'Joseph' in the dungeon who can interpret the king's dream... What looked like an overnight divine acceleration testimony was in fact preluded by a long waiting season.

Fourteen centuries later, Mordecai came on the scene and re-enacted a similar story with a seeming accelerated ending. In just one night, a troubled king who had terrible insomnia turned to reading the royal diary as a lullaby, runs into the record of how Mordecai had saved him a good while before then—possibly years—and he set in motion an accelerated series of events that culminated in this concluding testimony about Mordecai:

> *"Mordecai the Jew became the prime minister, with authority next to that of King Xerxes himself. He was very great among the Jews, who held him in*

high esteem, because he continued to work for the good of his people and to speak up for the welfare of all their descendants." (Esther 10:3 NLT)

He had saved a king's life in Esther Chapter 2. The king remembered in Esther Chapter 6. What the writer recorded five chapters apart—and chapters were not introduced to the narrative till about sixteen centuries after the story was originally written—was in fact, about a five-year gap.[1] It is historically and customarily unthinkable that someone that saved a monarch's life is left unrewarded—more so in Persia. That was why Xerxes naturally asked for what had been done to reward Mordecai when that part of the diary was read to him (Esther 6:3). He asked because he assumed something must have been done and his surprise at nothing having been done spurred him to take immediate (or *accelerated*) action. But again, in reality, Mordecai had been waiting for that for 5 years! At the end of the day, God—Who, by the way, was not mentioned throughout the book of Esther—manifested His invisible hand and brought Mordecai such an exceeding and a dramatic reward that saw his arch enemy elevated in his death upon the gallows originally planted for Mordecai.

What Jesus came to do for humanity was

---

[1] See the timeline through the book of Esther as presented in the New World Encyclopedia. "Esther, Book of—New World Encyclopedia", *New World Encyclopedia*, 2017 <http://www.newworldencyclopedia.org/entry/Esther,_Book_of#Timeline_of_Major_Events>.

accomplished in 3 days, but he waited for 3 decades before beginning His ministry (and all of humanity waited for 4 millennia for that to happen). Again and again, we find the same fabric through the scriptures.

In this book, I'll leave you with the five #peaces of thought that I left Lydia with, that when God seems to be missing in *inaction* as you keep waiting and waiting for Him to show up, you can find Him if you will lean in and behold:

God is in His agenda.

God is in His time.

God is in your trust.

God is in your perseverance.

And God is in your contentment.

They are simple #peaces of thought, but they are profound. They are like five tracks in an album on God's extravagant love. Such an album will contain countless tracks, but as with most albums, some tracks stand out and resonate deeply with us. We add them to 'favourites' and listen to them on repeat. I'm hoping these selected tracks will become like that for you.

If you are also going through a sort of *Lydia moment* (or know someone who is), hopefully, this encouragement we both received from our conversation can bring you (or them) some hope.

God says to tell you (in first person singular): "You are my hero!"

I think that's amazing!

"Hello Hero. Let's journey together."

Preface

Stella, the lady down the street is well-known for her promiscuity. 4 pregnancies, 3 abortions and 1 child—all out of wedlock. Christy on the other hand lives up the hill and is well-known for her chastity. She married Tom as a virgin. They've been married for a decade but yet to have a child. What the promiscuous was getting in unwanted successions, the faithful kept hoping and praying for. Every menstrual period is a painful reminder that God has left her prayer line on hold.

The Bible is filled with many stories of divine delays and white spaces. Why would God promise Abraham countless children but wait for so long before bringing him the son of promise? Why would He let Rachel wait for so long before Joseph was born? Why would He give Joseph a dream at seventeen never to be fulfilled till after a decade? Why wait till Moses is eighty before calling him to save a nation? And why call Paul and leave him to wander in the background for seventeen years before he was appointed as a missionary?[2]

J.D. Greear noted,

> After Mary became pregnant with the Messiah, God waited for several months to tell her fiancé, Joseph, about the miraculous conception. Why did God wait? During that delay, Joseph (naturally) assumed she had cheated on him (I mean, what else could you assume?). This means that for several months, Mary had to go through the humiliation of pregnancy alone with everyone, even her beloved fiancé, assuming she was a cheater. God chose to do it that way. Why? Why did He wait so long to tell Joseph? Why the "white space"?[3]

To be honest, you don't even have to look as far as the Bible to see examples of people that had been delayed, as it were, by God—you just need to look at the person in your mirror! Even life in its own right has a way with delays: flight delays, project execution delays, mail delivery delays—life is saturated with delays. But it's one thing to have a delayed flight or a delayed delivery which can be tracked online, and it's another thing entirely to be delayed by that which you could not track—that which you have no clue when

---

[2] See Galatians 1:17-19; 2:1; Acts 13:2
[3] J.D. Greear, "When You Can't Feel God", *FaithGateway*, 2015 <http://www.faithgateway.com/when-you-cant-feel-god>.

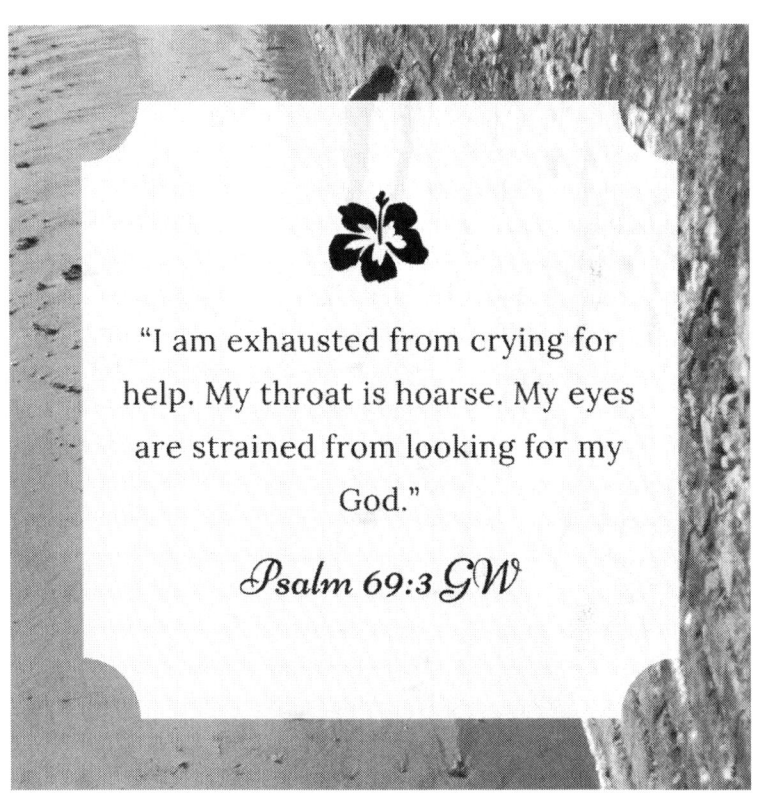

"I am exhausted from crying for help. My throat is hoarse. My eyes are strained from looking for my God."

Psalm 69:3 *GW*

exactly it will *be*. All of a sudden, God goes missing.

Sooner than later, people like Christy and Tom starts to learn the song of David...

> *"I am exhausted from crying for help.*
> *My throat is hoarse. My eyes are*
> *strained from **looking for my God.**"*
> *(Psalm 69:3 GW).*

The situation of our delay gets distilled into that singular question—**Where is God?** You've cried to Him from the stench of the putridity of your situation, and you thought He should know better and answer you speedily, but... silence. The palpable silence lingers so long and stays so thick that you could slice through it with a knife...

How do you go through painful waiting periods and still endeavour to keep the unity of your spirit, soul and body in His bond of peace? I believe that **peace is not the absence of delays, peace is the presence of God in your delay.** What you need to do is to locate God in the midst of your delay.

Peace is not the absence of delays, peace is the presence of God in your delay.

#WaitingCompass

Where is God in the delay?

#WaitingCompass

Track 1:
God is in His Agenda

"I MARRIED YOU!"

No, not "you", I mean her, the beautiful damsel whose stunning smile melted into my shoulder in the picture on the next page. Between the two of us though, "I Married You" isn't just a phrase; it's the title of the book I bought for her on the very first day I met her. It was in a Youth Service Camp in Northern Nigeria. I was drawn to her as she stood looking at the books at a book stand in front of the hall where I had just finished leading a Bible Study. I walked up to her, struck up a conversation, and felt *led* to buy her a book by Late Walter Trobisch.

I wanted to buy her "I Loved A Girl" which was the only book by that author which I had read at the time, but they were out of copies, so I opted for another title by the same author. And the title became a prophetic script: "I MARRIED YOU." Indeed, on the 27th of July, 2016, I married her. Besides, on the same day, she graduated with a first class in her LLB programme.

Let me back up a bit so you can get the gist.

When Eleos was leaving Nigeria for the UK in 2013, I intended to meet her at the airport. I woke up early enough, stopped by a store to buy her a golden wristwatch that I wanted to give her as a parting gift. I also intended to hand her the relationship journal where I had chronicled our first conversations in our first few months of courtship. However, Lagos traffic had other plans and I didn't make it to the airport in time to meet her. She had boarded the plane before I got there.

I cried. Like, literally.

I remember that the flight's take-off was delayed even after passengers had boarded. We spent those minutes of delay having a phone conversation until the flight was ready for take-off. The only thing I can remember in that long conversation, however, was this:

> *"Eleos, don't worry. I'll come and give you these things in the UK by myself..."*

I didn't mean a word of it, though. I had no plans of coming to the UK. For all I know, I didn't even have a Nigerian Passport at the time let alone a UK Visa...

Months later, in our almost-every-night conversations I find myself saying to her while trying to encourage her with regards to her studies:

> *"Don't worry. Study well and finish with a first class... I'll be there at your convocation and whisk you off to marry you on the same day."*

Again, it was just a joke, but I love to tease her with the idea...

Eventually, however, not only did I actually come to give her the golden wristwatch by myself but I also witnessed her graduation and *wifed* her the same day! It became a beautiful love story that went viral on the internet and turned a supposedly *quiet* wedding in Birmingham (with less than 50 people in attendance) into some news headline both within and beyond the UK.

That's not the full story, though. What I haven't mentioned is that this beautiful story was forged on the anvil of a long delay. My wife and I courted for 1,629 days! That's 4 years and 5 months of being in love and not being able to kiss or smooch the partner in whom your soul delights. (I know, we went for the high standard.) I don't know many millennials about our age who would wait that long. And if we are being honest, we didn't see ourselves waiting for that long before getting married either. However, life happened. The kind of divine opportunities that presented itself along our path brought both progress and physical distance away from each other. In love, we embraced it and enjoyed the roller coaster that ushered in July 27, 2016. In that long delay, a lot happened. The relationship went through various tests. The devil opened various doors of alternative engagements, but we remained together. Now, we can look back and see what God was up to all along. Our simple story became an inspiration for so many young people. We watched as hundreds of them approached us via social media asking for mentoring. Some of them were almost giving up on the possibility of a godly relationship before hearing our story and hope came alive in their hearts. The mentorship group is now over 1,500 people-strong. My wife and I have received messages from parents who made prayer points for their children out of our story.

All to the glory of God.

And that's the point, isn't it? God's agenda from eternity past to eternity future is singular: **the revelation of His glory**. The glory of God is the 'why' behind every testimony. And trust me, it looks awesome upon the canvas of life's delays.

Ask Mary and Martha. They "sent someone to tell Jesus, "Lord, the one you love is sick."… But when he heard that Lazarus was sick, he stayed where he was for two more days."[4] To the on-looker, that doesn't make so much sense. You hurry to help the one you love; but God delays to help the one He loves

---

[4] John 11:3,6 NCV

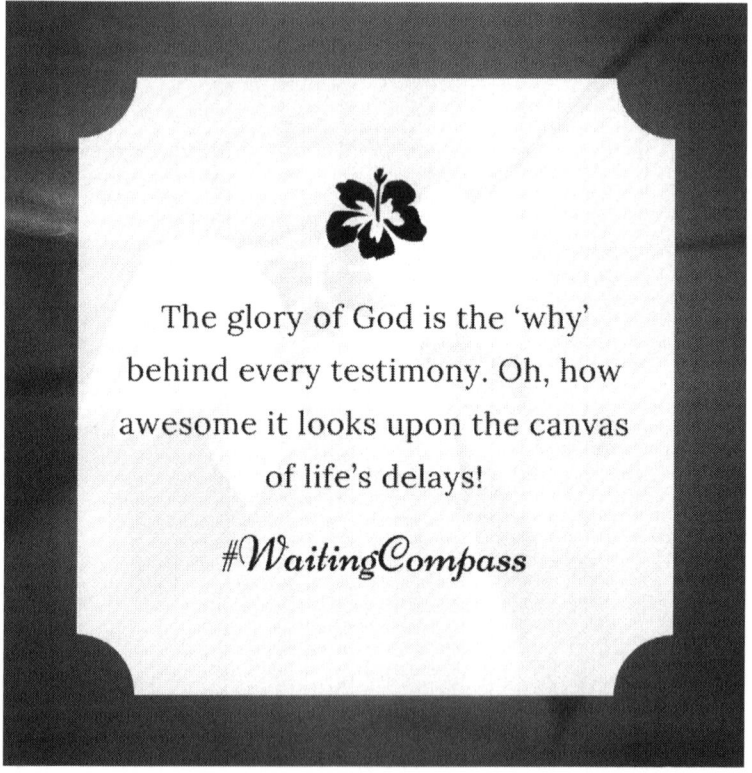

The glory of God is the 'why' behind every testimony. Oh, how awesome it looks upon the canvas of life's delays!

#WaitingCompass

so that His glory may be revealed in the full magnificence of its colours.

Yes, healing a sick man is a big deal, but definitely not as God-glorifying as raising a man who had been dead for four days. Jump down to the next chapter and we will begin to see why this was probably the most productive miracle of Jesus in all His three years of ministry.

> *"There had been many people with Jesus when he raised Lazarus from the dead and told him to come out of the tomb. Now they were telling others about what Jesus did. Many people went out to meet Jesus, because they had heard about this miracle. So the Pharisees said to each other, "You can see that nothing is going right for us. **Look! The whole world is following him.**""*
> (John 12:17-19 NCV)

Looking back to *before* and *after* the story of Lazarus, Jesus stated His agenda without mincing words. Quoting from the New Century Version:

> *[Before] "This sickness will not end in death. It is for the glory of God, **to bring glory to the Son of God.**" (11:4)*

> *[After] "Didn't I tell you that if you believed you would see **the glory of God?**" (11:40)*

"...we will be held in peace and not fall to pieces when we come to terms with the fact that He doesn't exist to bring us pleasure —we exist to give Him pleasure; and in so doing, we find our own pleasure."

#WaitingCompass

God delights in setting the stage for the revelation of His glory by the circumstances that Providence leads us into. God doesn't exist for you; you exist for Him—and that's good news! Often times, our frustrations in our dealings with God has everything to do with Him not meeting our needs as we expected Him to, but in actual fact, we will be held in peace and not fall to pieces when we come to terms with the fact that He doesn't exist to bring us pleasure—we exist to give Him pleasure; and in so doing, we find our own pleasure.

Mary and Martha wanted their brother to be healed—that's *their* agenda; Jesus wanted to raise a man from the dead—that's *His* agenda. So while they waited and then lamented at His absence, He was in fact hiding (in a manner of speaking) in His super-glorious agenda.

The same can be said of Rachel. She wanted a child at all means—that's her agenda; God wanted ten sons that will drive a beloved boy into the office of the prime minister (in their vehicle of hatred)—that's His agenda, and it's more glorious. Hannah hoped for a child year-in year-out, even when her husband wasn't complaining—that's her agenda. But God wanted a prophet that will pop on the scene just in time to transition from the fading priesthood of Eli's lineage—that's His agenda. We all want things; God wants His glory to be made known. That has been His agenda, and still is! Submit yours to Him.

"While we all want things; God wants His glory to be made known."

#WaitingCompass

The goal of prayer is not getting God to do what we want; it's **getting what we want to align with what He wants!** God says

> *"'I don't think the way you think. The way you work isn't the way I work."...For as the sky soars high above earth, so the way I work surpasses the way you work, and the way I think is beyond the way you think."*
> *(Isaiah 55:8-9 MSG)*

Therefore in your delay,

> *"Trust the Lord completely, and don't depend on your own knowledge. With every step you take, think about what he wants, and he will help you go the right way."*
> *(Proverbs 3:5-6 ERV).*

Plan and prepare and pray as much as you want, but after all is said and done, wrap your agenda in the blanket of His will—"Lord, not my will, but let Your will be done in my life." Think about what He wants!

So if your heavenly Father has chosen some delay for you, embrace it with thanksgiving. At some point, maybe He will give you what you ask for. And then again, maybe He wants to do something even more. Maybe the reason He says no to you today is because He has a big yes for you in the future that will surpass your wildest dreams… It's very much like Him! My wife and I definitely think so.

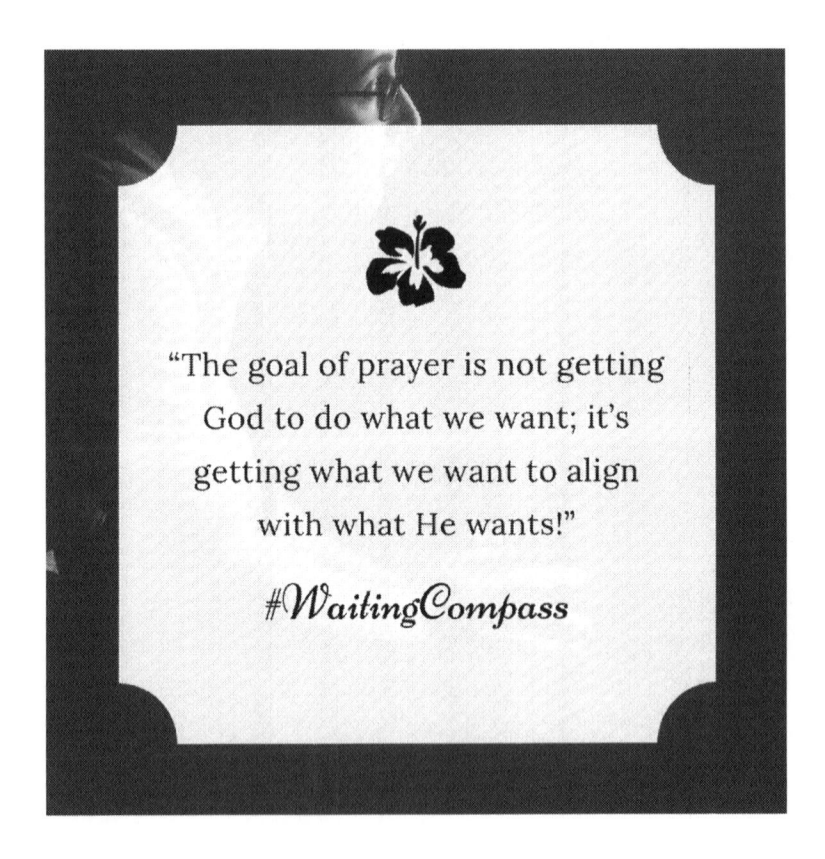

"The goal of prayer is not getting God to do what we want; it's getting what we want to align with what He wants!"

#WaitingCompass

Track 2:
God is in His Time

I kept checking my phone every five minutes. I confirmed that I'd taken the settings off 'silent mode'. I couldn't afford to miss the call when Tope calls. She had sent me a text earlier in the day to tell me another call-up batch list had been pasted at our alma mater's office of the Dean of Students' Affairs. She was in the university campus at the time and decided to head over to the DSA office and check if our names were among the list of graduated students that had been mobilised for the National Youth Service Corps—the second batch in the year. Tope is my colleague and we had both narrowly missed the first mobilisation batch, so we've prayed and were hopeful—certain, even—that our names will be among the second mobilisation batch.

The National Youth Service Corps is an almost compulsory and definitely essential part of the Nigerian education system. Being a graduate is not enough to get a good job; most organisations want to know you've gone through the NYSC programme before you can be gainfully employed. Tertiary institution graduates are therefore mobilised in three batches through the year all across the nation and posted to a different part of the country to serve the nation voluntarily beginning with a three-week somewhat para-military training camp experience. It is the one thing Nigerian graduates look forward to. For some, it will be their first time in a part of the country they would never otherwise have travelled to. And from a Christian point of view, since God's mission rides on the waves of migration, the NYSC scheme has also been an agent of revival and mission across the nation as vibrant Christian graduates are reshuffled across the nation, taking their exuberant faith expressions with them.

Understandably, Tope and I and hundreds of our colleagues that missed the first mobilisation in 2010 looked forward to the next.

She should have called by now.

I checked my phone again. Then I saw she had sent a text message. *How did I not hear the phone beep?* I clicked in a hurry and almost immediately, my excitement got deflated.

"Sorry, we've not been mobilised with this second batch either. Our names are not on the list. Checked three times."

To say that I became frustrated would be an understatement. I had to wait for another four months for the last mobilisation for the year. Since I had no choice, I waited. And waited. By the time the third mobilisation list was out, my name was not included either, but lots of my classmates were mobilised. That was when I got angry at God.

What's up, God? Have I done anything wrong? I prayed about this and I thought we had an agreement. Why are You going back on our deal? What's with the three-year plan You gave me in prayers last weekend if I'm not getting mobilised for NYSC now?

After processing my thoughts and allowing God's Spirit to speak through my disappointment, I picked up my pen and wrote a poem titled "I WILL WAIT". It's the poem I ended this book with.

To cut to the chase, I was delayed for over a year before I was eventually mobilised for NYSC. Eventually, I was posted to Gombe State in Northern Nigeria, 17 hours' drive away from home. No sooner had I arrived in the state than I heard amongst the Christian folks that GOMBE is actually an acronym for *God of My Beautiful Experience*. I thought that was a good play on words, but again, my Christian-mind was open to the prophetic tangent to that.

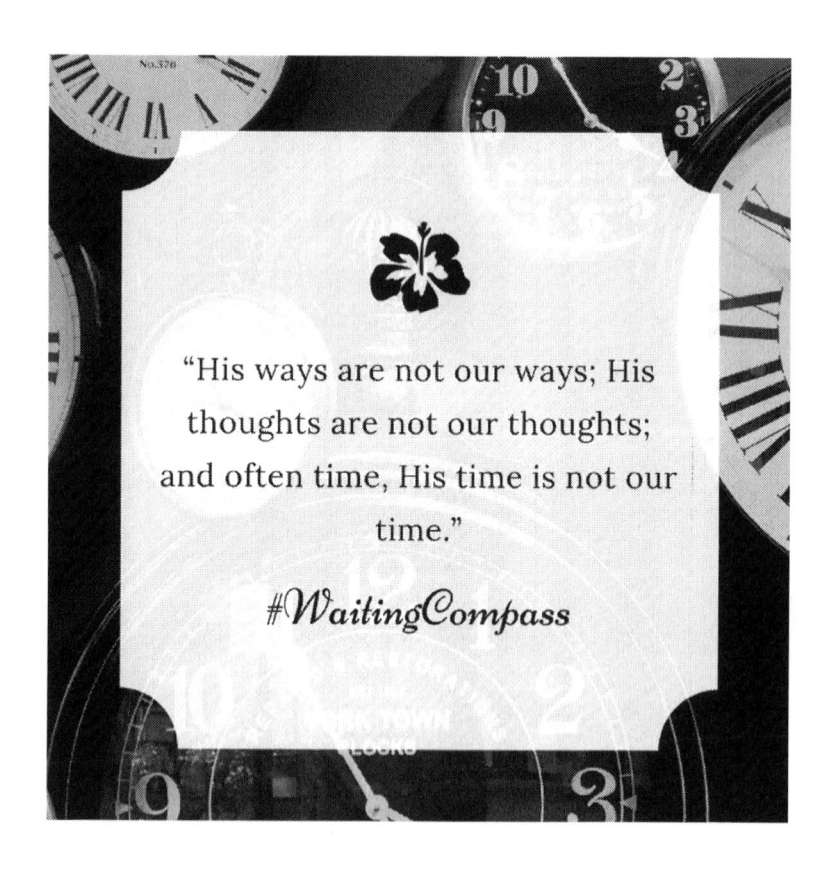

"His ways are not our ways; His thoughts are not our thoughts; and often time, His time is not our time."

#WaitingCompass

Few months into my service in the state, the story I started the last track with happened. I was drawn to Eleos as she was looking at a book at a book stand.

"I Married You."

And the rest, as they say, is history.

Today, I wake up each day to one of God's finest daughters by my side. If I had been mobilised for NYSC anytime earlier, that is what I would have missed, of course, amongst other *beautiful experiences* I had in Gombe State. I look back to that period of delay, no longer with frustration, but with great joy.

It's frustrating to be in a hurry when God isn't. In fact, God is never in a hurry. It's only natural for us to pray time-bound prayers when asking for His intervention in our life's situation, but we tend to forget that the God we serve is not bound by our time.

"God makes everything happen at the right time."
(Ecclesiastes 3:11 CEV).

Yes,

"we can never completely understand everything he does... yet, he does everything at just the right time."
(Ecclesiastes 3:11 ERV).

His ways are not our ways; His thoughts are not our thoughts; and often time, His time is not our time.

But while you wait in your delay,

> *"don't get tired...You will be rewarded **when the time is right**, if you don't give up."*
> *(Galatians 6:9 CEV)*

Matthew tells us an interesting story in his gospel account:

> *"...Jesus told his disciples to get into their boat and cross to the other side of the lake while he stayed to get the people started home. Then afterwards he went up into the hills to pray. Night fell, and out on the lake the disciples were in trouble. For the wind had risen and they were fighting heavy seas. About four o'clock in the morning Jesus came to them, walking on the water! They screamed in terror, for they thought he was a ghost."*
> *(Matthew 14:22-26 TLB)*

I can only imagine the disappointment and fear of the disciples when they were left alone on the high sea at the mercy of terrible storms while Jesus was nowhere to be found. Following the timeline of the events as recorded by Matthew, they battled with waves that were stronger than their experiences for no less than 6 hours, maybe 8. And in those hours they must have asked loads of questions—in fact, I think they probably came to the conclusion that He must have been dead, which could explain why they

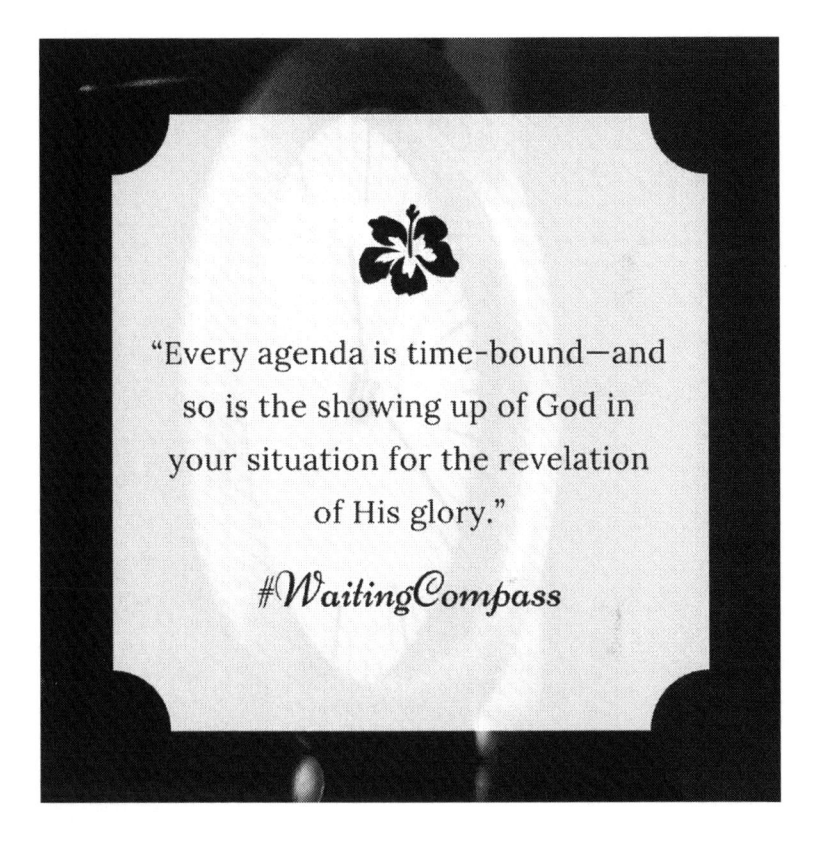

"Every agenda is time-bound—and so is the showing up of God in your situation for the revelation of His glory."

#WaitingCompass

thought He was a ghost when He eventually showed up.

Not only was Jesus hidden in His agenda (which, again, was the revelation of His glory as He walked on the water and even got Peter doing the same), but He was also hidden in His *timing*. Every agenda is time-bound—and so is the showing up of God in your situation for the revelation of His glory.

And isn't it reassuring to know that while we await His timely intervention according to His agenda, He's somewhere in the dark praying for us? While the waves rise and slap the twelve in their boat, Jesus was praying—praying for them. While they were asking "Where is He? He just fed countless thousands, won't He at least show up and help us?" He was busy praying. While they were thinking of the possibility that He might be dead, He was busy praying for them.

And He still does. Right "now he is on God's right side and is begging God for us."[5] He will show up just for you just in time!

Joyce Meyer writes:

> "God gives us hopes and dreams for certain things to happen in our lives, but He doesn't always allow us to see the exact timing of His plan. Although frustrating, not knowing the exact timing is often what keeps us in the program. There are times when we might give up if we knew how long it was going to take, but when we accept God's timing, we can learn to live in hope and enjoy our lives while God is working on our problems. We know

---

[5] Romans 8:34 ICB

that God's plan for our lives is good, and when we entrust ourselves to Him, we can experience total peace and happiness."[6]

And to be honest, it's okay not to know. When will the prophecy hanging over my life be fulfilled? When will I get pregnant? When will the promise be fulfilled? When will the dream come true? Listen to the Lord's refreshing response:

> *"The Father sets those dates...and they are not for you to know."*
> *(Acts 1:7 TLB).*

The point is this:

> *"If you are too eager, you will miss the road"*
> *(Proverbs 19:2 CEV).*

If there's anything you can be sure of regarding your impatience, be sure that your "impatience will get you into trouble."[7] But in the meantime,

> *"Rest in the Lord, wait patiently for him to act.... Don't fret and worry — it only leads to harm."*
> *(Psalm 37:7-8 TLB).*

---

[6] Joyce Meyer, "When God's Timing is Taking Too Long", *Joyce Meyer Ministries* <https://joycemeyer.org/everydayanswers/ea-teachings/when-gods-timing-is-taking-too-long>.
[7] Proverbs 19:2 GNT

"When will the promise be fulfilled? When will the dream come true?"
Listen to the Lord's refreshing response:
"The Father sets those dates...and they are not for you to know."
#WaitingCompass

Track 3:
God is in Your Trust

I couldn't resist smiling at my image in the mirror as I washed my hand in the toilet partly because of the thrill and pleasure of finding a release for the pressure that had built up in my internal organs over the long trip, and partly—in fact, majorly—because I was yet to recover from the miraculous provision that made the trip possible.

My wife and I had looked forward to the leadership conference since the moment we made up our mind to attend but the timing was 'financially wrong'. While the conference itself was free, there were other accompanying expenses which our budget couldn't accommodate including the hotel booking (since we had to arrive a night before the conference) and transport fare from Liverpool to Bradford.

The first miracle was that a pastor I was privileged to serve while in Bradford sent me a WhatsApp message just few days to the conference. It was a hotel booking confirmation—all-expense-paid. He has assured me that I have a home in Bradford, and all I needed to do was to let him know whenever we want to come over—and he kept his word. It became too late to change our mind. We've got to go for the conference and trust that the God that provided the accommodation will also provide the transport fare and even more so we could have enough for our living costs for the two days.

Eleos and I informed our neighbours and members in our congregation in Liverpool that we were traveling. We were sure we would go because we were persuaded that God will provide—but where the money would come from, we had no idea.

Just about that time, I'd shared a post on "taking responsibility for what we see" with the youths on Alive Mentorship Group—a mentoring club that my wife and I run online—so I reckoned it's another opportunity to live what we had preached. Rather than see lack and insufficiency, Eleos and I kept trying to intentionally maintain an attitude of thanksgiving in that phase.

As God would have it, a day before we were to leave for the conference, a sister reached out to me via a Facebook message. I didn't have her contact details but could tell it was a God-connection. In fact, till after she sent just what we needed for our transport fare, I kept referring to her in masculine pronouns (judging by her profile picture). To cut to the chase, transport fare was provided.

But then, there's still a little problem. After buying the coach tickets (which was what we could afford, as opposed to train tickets), what we had left was definitely not going to be enough to get us from the coach station in Bradford to the hotel and from the hotel to the venue of the conference the next day...but still, we set out.

Maybe at this point, you are wondering why we chose to want to embarrass ourselves... Maybe you are wondering, "why can't they just live within their means and stay put in Liverpool?" Good question. But as a pastor, I knew right from when I felt called into the pastoral ministry that my family and I would have to literally live by trusting God's ability if we are going to make any impact in our generation and beyond. Of course, there are pastors that live flamboyantly, but apparently, God did not call us to that track. As such, right from the genesis of our relationship as would-be couple till that February moment five years down the line, the story of our lives—my wife and I—had been an unending roller-coaster of the highs and lows of trusting God, and God had built a reputation of faithfulness over the years that gave us a surge of confidence in that phase of our lives. The many repetitions of how He had come through for us had earned Him a reputation that we could not shake off. We have transcended the acknowledgement of His ability to do things to also acknowledge that even if He doesn't, He is yet too faithful to fail. It was upon the anvil of the track record of His faithfulness that this experience was shaped. We were so sold out in our trust in Him that earlier on the same day, we booked for an item we needed at home to be delivered in two days (after we must have returned from the Bradford trip) on a pay-on-delivery terms—with nothing in the account save an unshakable persuasion that God will provide—and He did. So, no, we were not being foolish; we were judging God faithful knowing that if He did it before, He could do it again.

As we were heading for the coach station in Liverpool, my pregnant wife felt some peculiar hunger pangs, such as could be satisfied *only* by a buffet take-out from a Chinese restaurant—and not from just any Chinese restaurant but from a particular one that is arguably the most popular and most expensive Chinese restaurant in the City Centre.

I did what any supportive husband and father-in-embryo would do for his beautiful wife and soon-to-be mother of their child. "I'll get it for you" I said, as we approached the City Centre in a bus. What my mouth said and what my mind was thinking at the time didn't quite align, but I chose to ignore the thoughts and went quiet.

Silence.

More silence.

Suddenly, we both broke the silence simultaneously as we spontaneously started singing a song of thanksgiving and assurance in God's ability—the same song at that! It was another God-moment that reassured us that we would not be put to shame and that a beautiful testimony was in the offing.

We went to the restaurant and she went ahead to pick everything she wanted. I counted all the money we had left. It was just enough to pay for her food. By implication, if nothing happens between that moment and when we arrive at Bradford Interchange, we would be stranded. Literally.

As she was moving from dish to dish serving herself, I felt a prompting. "Check your account balance." I resisted. I was sure I knew how much I had in my account and wouldn't desire an embarrassing reminder. Then I felt it again, so I checked. And wouldn't you believe it, the account had been credited with a £100 thirteen minutes earlier. My eyes brightened. (By the way, from all indication, thirteen minutes earlier would be just about the time my wife and I did burst into that spontaneous praise song; our Spirit was being grateful for what God was doing at that very point in time. We just didn't know it yet tangibly.)

I showed my wife the alert, and the story changed. With springs in our steps and new songs on our lips, we set out for an exciting trip.

There was a mystery to the credit alert, though. It wasn't an online bank transfer from one account to another. The account statement showed that someone did enter a bank and made a cash deposit into my account, but there was no name in the transaction details; all it said was "EASTHAM D2."

Understandably, I was scared of touching the money at first. "What if someone *mistakenly* paid into my account? What if someone sent it to me so that I could help him transfer it to someone else?"—the questions kept coming. But I felt a reassuring whisper from God, "You asked; I've given. Enjoy!"

Looking back to the series of events that led to that, it almost seemed like God sent an angel to credit the account (of course, without our awareness) and then planted a peculiar hunger in my pregnant wife's belly to see where our trust lies. Thankfully, I think we passed that test.

****

On the flip side of putting our trust in God is what may seem to us as an unhappy ending, judging by our view from where we stand on the timeline to trace the narrative. Such is the story of Adoniram Judson.

In 1812, Adoniram Judson and his new bride, Nancy, left their familiar and comfortable New England surroundings to take the gospel to far-off Burma. After a difficult four-month voyage, they arrived in India only to hear discouraging reports about Burma and to learn that they could not stay in India. They spent a year moving from India to Mauritius (off the coast of South Africa) and back, to avoid deportation. Finally, against all advice, they managed to get aboard a ship heading for Burma. En route, Nancy gave birth to a stillborn child and almost died herself.

They finally arrived in Rangoon and began the arduous task of learning Burmese. They found the Burmese people to be committed to Buddhism and totally uninterested in and opposed to Christianity. The only other English-speaking couple in Rangoon left, leaving the Judsons alone to struggle with the language and the mission. The birth of a son brightened their lives, but when he was eight-months-old, he became ill. With no medicine or doctors in Rangoon, the baby died. The Judsons buried him in their backyard and plodded on through their tears.

After six years, they finally baptized their first convert. A handful more trickled in over the years, but mostly, they faced fierce opposition from the Buddhist monks and the government. In 1824, the British went to war against Burma, and Judson was arrested, tortured, and imprisoned on false charges as a spy. The conditions and torture in the prison were terrible. As he suffered with fever in that dark prison, Judson's wife delivered a letter from a friend that asked, "Judson, how's the outlook?" He replied, "The outlook is as bright as the promises of God."

Judson later was released from prison only to face the deaths of his wife and his two-year-old daughter. He fought intense depression and struggled against numerous setbacks. But he plodded on in faith until he died at age 62.

Today, over 600,000 Burmese Christians trace their roots back to Adoniram Judson, a man who trusted in God.[8]

****

The common denominator to stories of trusting God is acknowledgement of God's love for us, His limitless power and His unfailing willingness to come through for us. Yes, sometimes we strain and strain looking into the cloudy horizon and wondering, "is God really there?" "Is He really leading us into this fog?" "What's on the other side?" "Is there, even, an 'other side'?" At times like that, we need to preserve that dual knowledge that the Almighty and infinitely powerful God **loves** us and is **more-than-willing** to help us through our seeming delay, and our attitude will change while it lasts.

---

[8] Steven J. Cole, "Lesson 64: God's Delays (Acts 24:24-27)", *Bible.org*, 2013 <https://bible.org/seriespage/lesson-64-god-s-delays-acts-2424-27>.

"Trusting God is simply believing that He loves you, He's good, He has the power to help you, He wants to help you, and He will help you."

Joyce Meyer

In my walk with God over the years, I have found out that it takes an absolute trust in God to get an absolute care from God. The three Hebrews (Daniel's friends) can tell you that! Here's the drama that unfolded as recorded in Daniel 3:14-19 as Eugene Peterson paraphrased it in The Message.

The Challenge...

Nebuchadnezzar asked, "Is it true, Shadrach, Meshach, and Abednego, that you don't respect my gods and refuse to worship the gold statue that I have set up? I'm giving you a second chance—but from now on, when the big band strikes up you must go to your knees and worship the statue I have made. If you don't worship it, you will be pitched into a roaring furnace, no questions asked. **Who is the god who can rescue you from my power?**"

Their Absolute Trust...

Shadrach, Meshach, and Abednego answered King Nebuchadnezzar, "Your threat means nothing to us. If you throw us in the fire, the God we serve can rescue us from your roaring furnace and anything else you might cook up, O king. **But even if he doesn't**, it wouldn't make a bit of difference, O king. We still wouldn't serve your gods or worship the gold statue you set up."

The King's Worst.

Nebuchadnezzar, his face purple with anger, cut off Shadrach, Meshach, and Abednego. He ordered the furnace fired up seven times hotter than usual. He ordered some strong men from the army to tie them up, hands and feet, and throw them into the roaring furnace. Shadrach, Meshach, and Abednego, bound hand and foot, fully dressed from head to toe, were pitched into the roaring fire.

God's Absolute Care...

Because the king was in such a hurry and the furnace was so hot, flames from the furnace killed the men who carried Shadrach, Meshach, and Abednego to it, while the fire raged around Shadrach, Meshach, and Abednego. Suddenly King Nebuchadnezzar jumped up in alarm and said, "Didn't we throw three men, bound hand and foot, into the fire?" "That's right, O king," they said. "But look!" he said. "I see four men, walking around freely in the fire, completely unharmed! And the fourth man looks like a son of the gods!"

The divine agenda fulfilled...

Nebuchadnezzar went to the door of the roaring furnace and called in, "Shadrach, Meshach, and Abednego, servants of the High God, come out here!" Shadrach, Meshach, and Abednego walked out of the fire. All the important people, the government leaders and king's counsellors, gathered around to examine them and discovered that the fire hadn't so much touched the three men—not a hair singed, not a scorch mark on their clothes, not even the smell of fire on them! Nebuchadnezzar said, "Blessed be the

God of Shadrach, Meshach, and Abednego! He sent his angel and rescued his servants who trusted in him! They ignored the king's orders and laid their bodies on the line rather than serve or worship any god but their own.

"Therefore I issue this decree: Anyone anywhere, of any race, colour, or creed, who says anything against the God of Shadrach, Meshach, and Abednego will be ripped to pieces, limb from limb, and their houses torn down. **There has never been a god who can pull off a rescue like this.**" (Daniel 3:14-19 MSG)

****

Don't miss the point here. The agenda was not to rescue the three Hebrews; the agenda was to get the king to acknowledge the King of kings and enforce His worship throughout the land—talk about the revelation of the glory of God.

So because of the agenda, God had to delay… He didn't rescue the three Hebrews before they were thrown into the fire. Rather, He waited till the intensity of the fire was multiplied—till servants of the king died attesting to the potency and intensity of the fire. He even waited till His three children were cast into the fire…then He shows up.

So where's God in their delay? Yes, He's in His agenda; yes, He's in His timing; but most especially, He's in their trust. Had they not come to the **even-if-He-doesn't** threshold in their faith—which is the

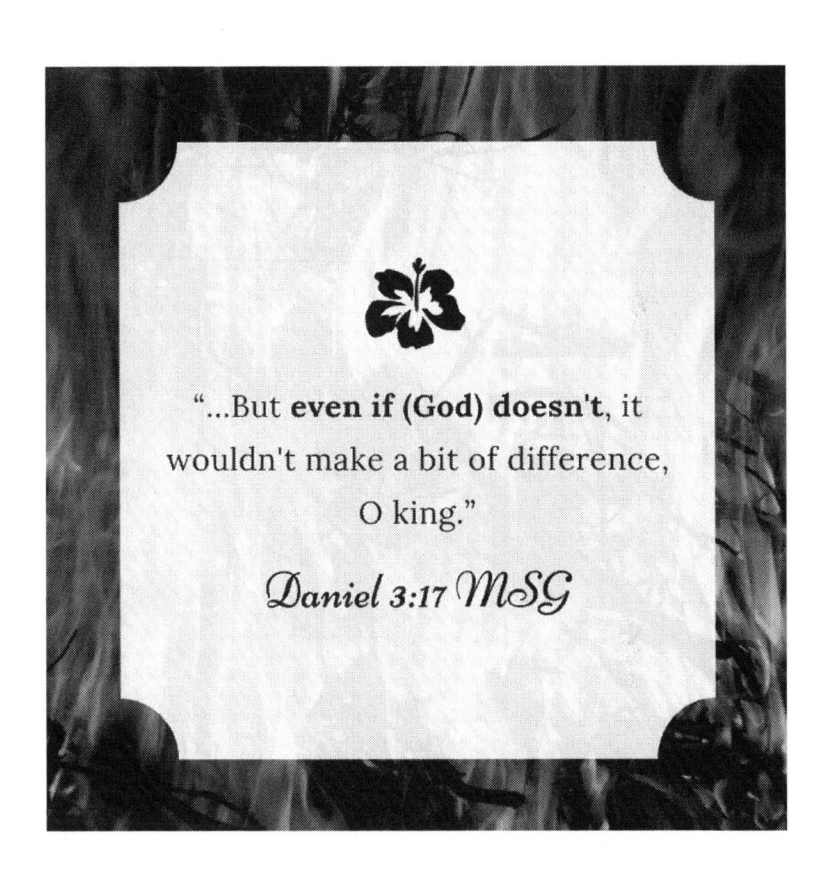

"...But **even if (God) doesn't**, it wouldn't make a bit of difference, O king."

Daniel 3:17 MSG

threshold of trust—God wouldn't even have the opportunity to show up as He did and the agenda would have been short-circuited.

Don't miss the point here. The agenda was not to rescue the three Hebrews; the agenda was to get the king to acknowledge the King of kings and enforce His worship throughout the land—talk about the revelation of the glory of God.

So because of the agenda, God had to delay… He didn't rescue the three Hebrews before they were thrown into the fire. Rather, He waited till the intensity of the fire was multiplied—till servants of the king died attesting to the potency and intensity of the fire. He even waited till His three children were cast into the fire…then He shows up.

So where's God in their delay? Yes, He's in His agenda; yes, He's in His timing; but most especially, He's in their trust. Had they not come to the **even-if-He-doesn't** threshold in their faith—which is the threshold of trust—God wouldn't even have the opportunity to show up as He did and the agenda would have been short-circuited.

Don't allow anything tamper with your trust—that's the unfailing zone of God's intervention. When you come to the even-if-He-doesn't zone, the game changes!

Even if He doesn't give me a child… Even if He doesn't heal me… Even if He doesn't provide for the bills to be paid… and, as Job radically proclaimed, "Even if God kills me, I have hope in him".[9]

---

[9] Job 13:15 NCV

Your trust is the unfailing zone of God's intervention. When you come to the **even-if-He-doesn't zone**, the game changes!

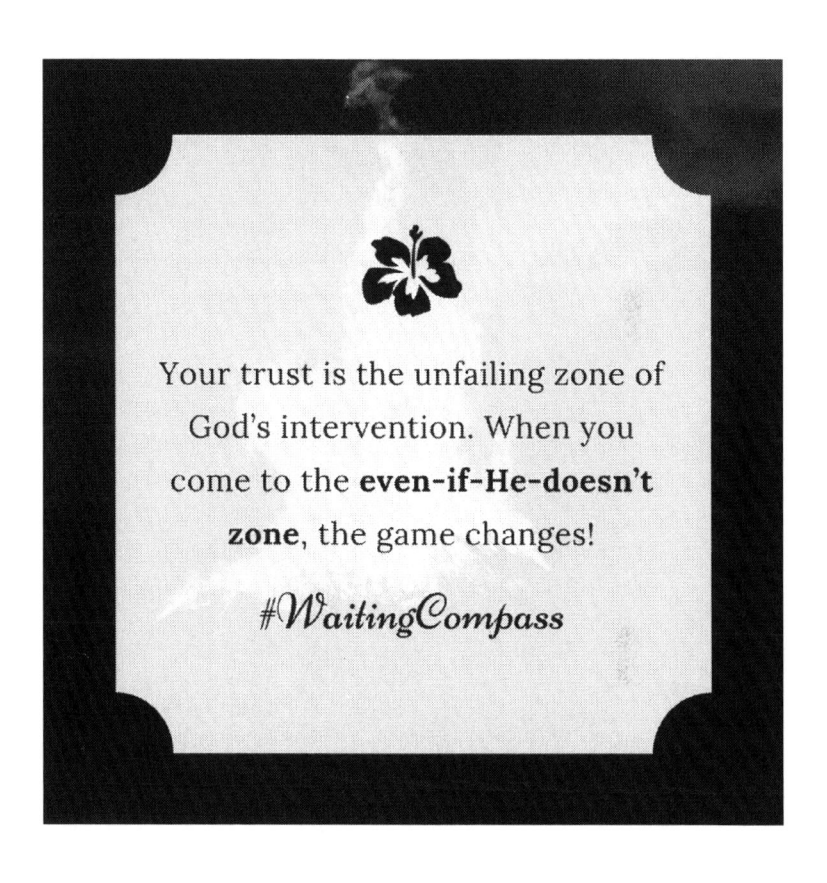

#WaitingCompass

Job believed that and God showed up for him. The three Hebrews believed that and God showed up for them. Adoniram Judson believed that, and God caused Him to outlive his life. My wife and I believed that and God came through for us. You will be in good company if you believe the same.

God, through the many repetitions of His power, love and faithfulness in the scriptures, has built a reputation that we can trust. The only way we can miss that is to put our trust in a fellow man.

> *"Cursed is the man who puts his trust in mortal man and turns his heart away from God."*
> *(Jeremiah 17:5 TLB)*

> *"It is better to trust the Lord than to put confidence in men. It is better to take refuge in him than in the mightiest king!"*
> *(Psalm 118:8-9 TLB)*

> *"Don't trust anyone— not your best friend or even your wife!"*
> *(Micah 7:5 NLT)*

> *"But we suffered so that we would stop trusting ourselves and learn to trust God, who brings the dead back to life."*
> *(2 Corinthians 1:9 GW)*

God still provides. He still moves stones. He has sent His angels to minister to His sons and daughters. He still plants visions in people's hearts and plants provisions in people's bank accounts... And surely, He still tests our loyalties and trust.

Don't give up on God. He won't give up on you.

****

To conclude the story we started with about God's miraculous provision, not until 3 or 4 days after did we discover who the 'angel of God' was. It was a kind mother in Nigeria. She had credited a client that helps her with cross-national transactions with the naira equivalent of £100 and instructed the client to send the pounds equivalent to my account. My wife and I had hosted this godly woman and her husband briefly on their previous visit to the UK. They are more or less like parents to us, but...imagine the timing! It's amazing what God can set in motion in another part of the world just by the reason of your trust. God still makes provision; more so when we live within His vision for our lives.

Trust Him. Always!
God is in His agenda.
God is in His timing.
God is in your trust.
And next, God is in your perseverance.

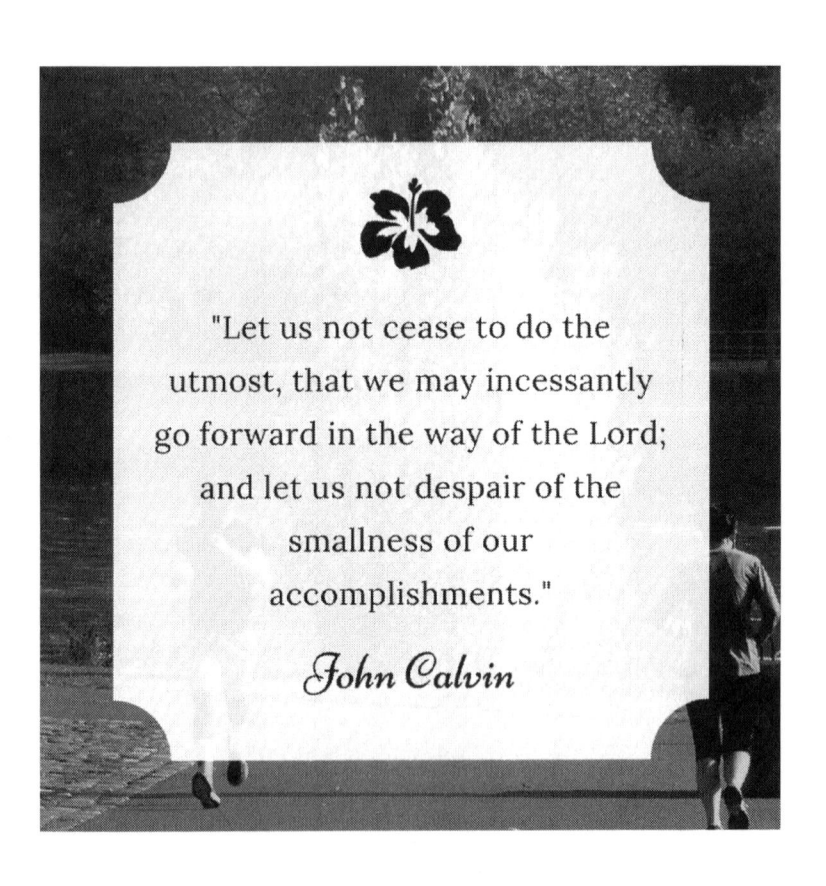

"Let us not cease to do the utmost, that we may incessantly go forward in the way of the Lord; and let us not despair of the smallness of our accomplishments."

John Calvin

Track 4:

God is in Your Perseverance

> "By perseverance the snail reached the ark."—C.H. Spurgeon

From the booklet Bits and Pieces comes an interesting story about Florence Chadwick, the first woman to swim the English Channel in both directions. On the Fourth of July in 1951, she attempted to swim from Catalina Island to the California coast. The challenge was not so much the distance, but the bone-chilling waters of the Pacific. To complicate matters, a dense fog lay over the entire area, making it impossible for her to see land. After about 15 hours in the water, and within a half mile of her goal, Chadwick gave up. Later she told a reporter, "Look, I'm not excusing myself. But if I could have seen land, I might have made it."

Not long afterward she attempted the feat again. Once more a misty veil obscured the coastline and she couldn't see the shore. But this time she made it because she kept reminding herself that land was there. With that confidence she bravely swam on and achieved her goal. In fact, she broke the men's record by 2 hours![10]

How many people were inches away to their divine intervention and then gave up on God. It's a sad thing. It takes perseverance to reach that haven of fulfilment. On the bridge of perseverance, Joseph crawled into his destiny. On the same bridge, David fought his way into his anointed responsibility. Hannah persevered through one more Shiloh convention and then her story changed. And Job. He rode the bicycle of trust on the wheels of perseverance before he found himself back in the familiar zone of God's blessings—but infinitely more this time.

Our lives are in the hands of God like a bow and arrow in the hands of an archer. Often times, God is aiming at something we cannot see, but He continues to stretch and strain, and every once in a while we feel like we can't take any more. Yet God pays no

---

[10] "Perseverance", *Sermon Illustrations*, 1989
<http://www.sermonillustrations.com/a-z/p/perseverance.htm>.

attention; He goes on stretching until His purpose is in sight, and then—just then—He lets the arrow fly.

****

It was the summer Olympics of 1992. It was the quarter finals of the 400 metre sprint. British athlete Derek Redmond was one of the favourites for the gold medal. A lifetime of training had brought him to this moment. The starters gun fired and the athletes burst out of the blocks.

Halfway through the race Derek Redmond was leading. Then disaster struck. His hamstring went and he collapsed on the track. The agony on his tear streaked face was both physical and mental. It was a crushing blow.

Medical attendants ran to assist him. Derek waved them away. He came to race and he was going to finish. He got to his feet and started hobbling down the track.

The crowd was mesmerised. Officials didn't know what to do. And then an older man ran onto the track. He brushed off officials who tried to stop him. He ran up beside Derek and placed his arms around him.

The man was Derek Redmond's father, Jim.

"You don't have to do this son" Jim said.

"Yes I do" Derek replied.

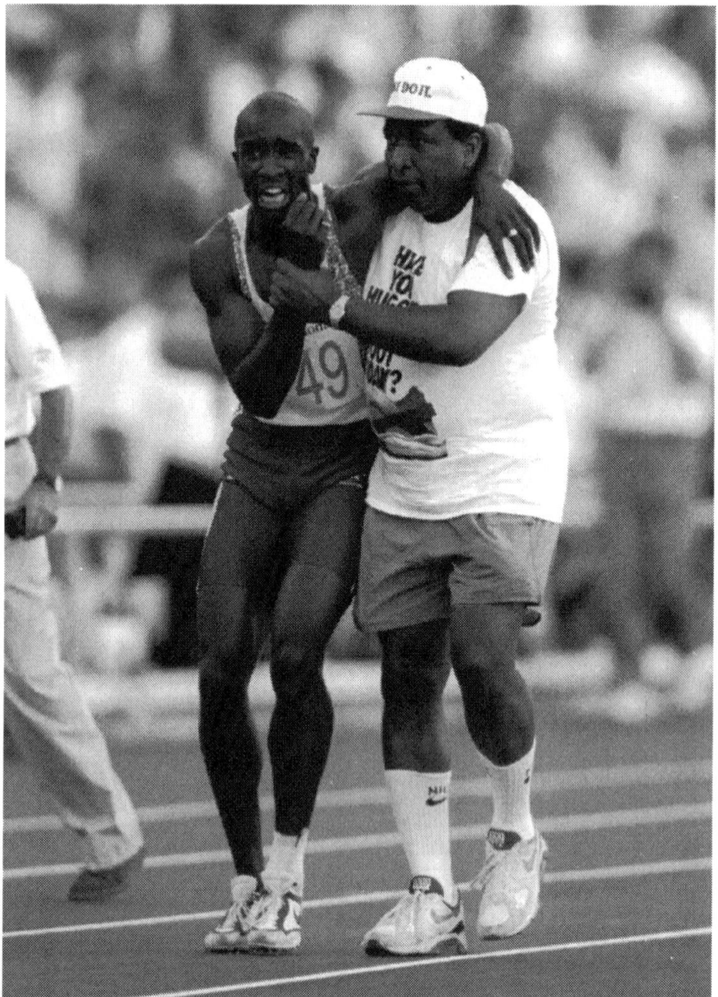
49

"Then we'll finish this race together" came the response from Derek's father.

Arm in arm, with agony on Derek's face, tears on his father's, Derek and Jim continued down the track. Derek buried his face in his father's shoulder. His father's strong shoulders carried his son physically and emotionally. Jim waved away officials who tried to stop them.

Finally, accompanied by a now roaring crowd, standing on their feet and applauding, Derek Redmond crossed the line. It became the defining moment of the Barcelona Olympics.[11]

---

[11] "Derek Redmond finishes at the Olympics", *Stories for Preaching* <http://storiesforpreaching.com/derek-redmond-finishes-at-the-olympics/>.

"Derek never won an Olympic medal...but he finished the race!"

#WaitingCompass

At that moment when disaster struck, he literally saw his dream crash before his eyes; his coach said he asked God, "Why? What has Derek done to deserve this?" And his Dad left his camera with his friend sitting next to him and ran to the field to be there for his son.

Derek never won an Olympic medal…but he finished the race! With his father by his side, he persevered to the very end and got a louder cheer than the gold medallist got. All of a sudden, who won the race didn't matter; what mattered was who *finished* the race.

Hearing Derek retell that story in an interview few years back when he returned to that same Olympic Stadium on that same track, he made it clear that his first attempt after the hamstring tore was to still get up and catch up with the opponents, who by then were just about 100 meters from the finish line. But after limping a few paces and looking ahead again, he saw that the other opponents had finished the race—at that point, his singular goal became to finish the race. At the end of the interview, in his own words, he said "the pain was temporary, but the glory remains".

What Derek didn't know was that the pain of that experience was going to become the canvas upon which his fulfilment in life was to be formed. Now, he's a motivational speaker with such an incredible gifting that everyone that listens to him feels like he's speaking directly to them. That's how gifted he is! And besides, he has lived what he now teaches. Don't

❀

"the pain was temporary, but the glory remains..."

#WaitingCompass

give up.

What Derek didn't know was that the pain of that experience was going to become the canvas upon which his fulfilment in life was to be formed. Now, he's a motivational speaker with such an incredible gifting that everyone that listens to him feels like he's speaking directly to them. That's how gifted he is! And besides, he has lived what he now teaches. Don't give up.

> *"You need to persevere so that when you have done the will of God, you will receive what he has promised."*
> *(Hebrews 10:36 NIV)*

Don't be like the Israelites. Most of them left the cross country race into the Promised Land half way because they lacked perseverance. At some point in their journey,

> *"They said to each other, "Let's choose a leader and go back to Egypt.""*
> *(Numbers 14:4 NCV).*

They gave up on God's promise in the cell of their delay;

> *"they quickly forgot what he had done; they did not wait for his advice."*
> *(Psalm 106:13 NCV).*

Don't let that be you. You are a believer, so live like one. Live in the full awareness of the eternal life you have received.

And talking of eternal life, Oswald Chambers said "The real meaning of eternal life is a life that can face anything it has to face without wavering. If we will take this view, life will become one great romance—a glorious opportunity of seeing wonderful things all the time." So true!

Despite being afflicted with rheumatism and migraine headaches, John Calvin still preached, wrote books, and governed Geneva, Switzerland, for 25 years. Somewhere in the midst of all that, he said these words:

> *"Let us not cease to do the utmost, that we may incessantly go forward in the way of the Lord; and let us not despair of the smallness of our accomplishments."*

John Wesley gave an excerpt from his diary as recorded by himself:

> Sunday, A.M., May 5: Preached in St. Anne's. Was asked not to come back anymore.
>
> Sunday, P.M., May 5: Preached in St. John's. Deacons said "Get out and stay out."
>
> Sunday, A.M., May 12: Preached in St. Jude's. Can't go back there, either.
>
> Sunday, A.M., May 19: Preached in St. Somebody Else's. Deacons called special meeting and said I

couldn't return.

Sunday, P.M., May 19: Preached on street. Kicked off street.

Sunday, A.M., May 26: Preached in meadow. Chased out of meadow as bull was turned loose during service.

Sunday, A.M., June 2: Preached out at the edge of town. Kicked off the highway.

Sunday, P.M., June 2: Afternoon, preached in a pasture. **10,000 people came out to hear me.**[12]

I could go on and on giving examples, but guess whose story can be added to this gallery of persevering icons? Ours! Let us wake up each morning and say to ourselves:

"The Lord will fulfill his purpose for
me"
(Psalm 138:8 ESV).

And keep living in the reality of the hope of His promises. Therein lies His help.

---

[12] "Perseverance", *Sermon Illustrations*, 1989
<http://www.sermonillustrations.com/a-z/p/perseverance.htm>.

Track 5:

God is in Your Contentment

What you have in God right now is much more than what you are yet to have in life.

When will you be happy?

When all is said and done—you've acknowledged that God is up to something with His glorious agenda concerning your life; you are not in doubt that He will make all things beautiful in His time; you have come to trust His unshakable promises and you are willing to keep hoping in perseverance—what do you do in the meantime? Or to probe a bit further, how would you fill in this blank: "I will be happy when _____"?

****

"Who ate Dele's food?"

Silence.

The Nursery 1 classroom was as quiet as a grave yard. Mrs Yusuf shouted the question a second time, so loud that I died inside, but I kept mute.

"Who ate Dele's food?!"

Still no response.

I can't remember how the episode ended, but I remember how it started…over two decades ago. I was in Nursery 1—fresh out of Pre-Nursery school. The class tradition was that each pupil that came to school with a food flask dropped the food flask inside a wooden trough constructed for that purpose at the back of the classroom. During the lunch break, each pupil went for his or her flask, took a seat, joined the rest of the class to chorus a prayer over the food, invited "Aunty" to 'come and eat' and banished Satan to go away. Aunty always replied "thank you", but Satan? I don't know. Perhaps, he stayed behind on that fateful day.

For whatever reason, I didn't come with a food flask that day. The sight of other pupils' food flasks at the back of the classroom aroused my appetite. The lure was too great to resist. So during the lunch break, I joined the rush to the wooden trough and picked a rather big food flask. I took a seat, joined the chorus, invited Aunty, but forgot to send Satan away. I sat and ate the rice and beans, fully conscious that the food belonged to someone else. I finished the food and returned an empty flask to the trough. My desire was satisfied, and it seemed at first that I pulled through successfully.

Minutes later, the dumb that owned the flask finally came to his senses, went for his flask but met it empty. He called Aunty's attention to it and she investigated the mishap. I was the last suspect. In fact, Mrs Yusuf asked me if I took note of the person that picked the flask while I went to the trough for *my* food. I was tempted to accuse someone else, but I turned down the urge and simply said "No."

That's how much I could remember about the incident and that became my first memorable act on the world stage of WANT. Unfortunately, many never leave that stage and keep up with unending acts and scenes of wants and more wants. The stage becomes a prison and on the production crew are the likes of lust, covetousness and discontent. Most inmates never leave.

Don't get me wrong, the impulse for wanting is absolutely legit—it is a very necessary part of being human. Without it, people would be inactive and unmotivated. So, we *want* a spouse that loves us, and a car that is fuel efficient and a job we enjoy and a child that is obedient and a healing that is permanent—add to that an internet connection that is at rocket speed—and the list goes on and on.

"Where did we get the idea that for there to be so much pain in the world—or in our world—God must have taken a leave of absence? We definitely did not get that from God's Word."

#WaitingCompass

It is also true of humans, however, that naturally, we tend to desire more than we need—a mistake you will hardly find plants or animals making. We always want something 'er'—something bigg*er*, nic*er*, fast*er*, or thinn*er*. And we always want "just a little more". We bought into the lie that without what we want—or as Christians, what we are *waiting on God for*—we are incomplete. Who told us that a family is incomplete without children? Who told us that every believer that falls ill will be healed? Who told us that God has gone to sleep when a beloved relative dies? Where did we get the idea that for there to be so much pain in the world—or in *our* world—God must have taken a leave of absence? We definitely did not get that from God's Word. Perhaps, the movie director on the stage of *want* wants his recruits to add that to the convoluted script he gives them to act.

In Andy Stanley's recent book, *Irresistible,* he writes:

> A renowned New Testament scholar recently acknowledged he lost his faith and embraced atheism because of suffering in the world. But the foundation of our faith is not a world without suffering. Pain and suffering don't disprove the existence of God. It only disproves the existence of a god who doesn't allow pain and suffering. Whose god is that? Not ours. Ours promised it.[13]

Could it be that the reason behind what we are waiting on God for is more about self-affirmation or

---

[13] Andy Stanley, *Irresistible* (Zondervan, 2018), p. 18.

living the life we've seen others live rather than the life in God's glorious agenda for ours? That would be covetousness, wouldn't it?

The terrible thing about coveting is that it is a seed sin; it opens the gate for more sins. I coveted someone else's lunch, and so I stole, and lied. Eve and Adam coveted the forbidden fruit and all of humanity fell in one giant swoop (Genesis 3:6). Gehazi coveted, lied and clinched a generational leprosy! (2 Kings 5:22-25). Achan coveted, stole and orchestrated a generational burial (Joshua 7:21-26). Page after page, the Bible tells us where coveting leads.[14] Yet, it is hard in our culture to be content with what we have.

One of the biggest lessons I am learning is that "What I have in God is greater than what I don't have in life." I read that first from Max Lucado's *Traveling Light* a decade ago, but it has stayed with me ever since and I have found that to be true in my personal experience. I've learned that "Naked a man comes from his mother's womb, and as he comes, so he departs. He takes nothing from his labour that he can carry in his hand".[15] I've learned that "Life is not defined by what you have, even when you have a lot".[16] I've learned that "The LORD does not look at the things man looks at. Man looks at the outward

---

[14] Both the Old and New Testaments point out that coveting is the root of many forms of sin, including lying (2 Kings 5:22-25), theft (Joshua 7:21), domestic troubles (Proverbs 15:27), murder (Ezekiel 22:12), lust (1 Timothy 6:9), greed (Proverbs 1:19), envy (Titus 3:3), and jealousy (1 Corinthians 3:3). These are all manifestations of an uncontrolled desire to acquire.

[15] Ecclesiastes 5:15 NIV

[16] Luke 12:15 MSG

appearance, but the Lord looks at the heart".[17] Heaven does not know you as the mother of two kids—or none. God doesn't see you as the healthy young man or as the Christian suffering with cancer or the kid with autism. When God thinks of you, He may see your compassion, your devotion, your tenderness or quick mind, but He doesn't think of your possessions. And when you think of you, you shouldn't either. If you define yourself by what you have—your kids, your good health, your well-paying job, your spouse, and your material possessions, you will only feel good when those things are intact and when you have more and more of them. But what happens when either of these things is missing?

Back to the question I started with, how would you complete the statement: "I will be happy when _____"? When I am healed? When I am promoted? When I am married? When I am pregnant? How would you finish that statement? What is the one thing separating you from joy right at this moment?

Now, with your answer firmly in mind, let's take it further. What if that ship never sails? What if the situation never changes? What if that dream never comes true? Could you still be happy? If not, then you will find it difficult while you wait because you are still starring on the stage of *want*. Wanting and waiting may have similar spellings, but they make a difficult couple. With few #peaces of questions, stories and thoughts below, let us reclaim our joy together.

---

[17] 1 Samuel 16:7 NIV

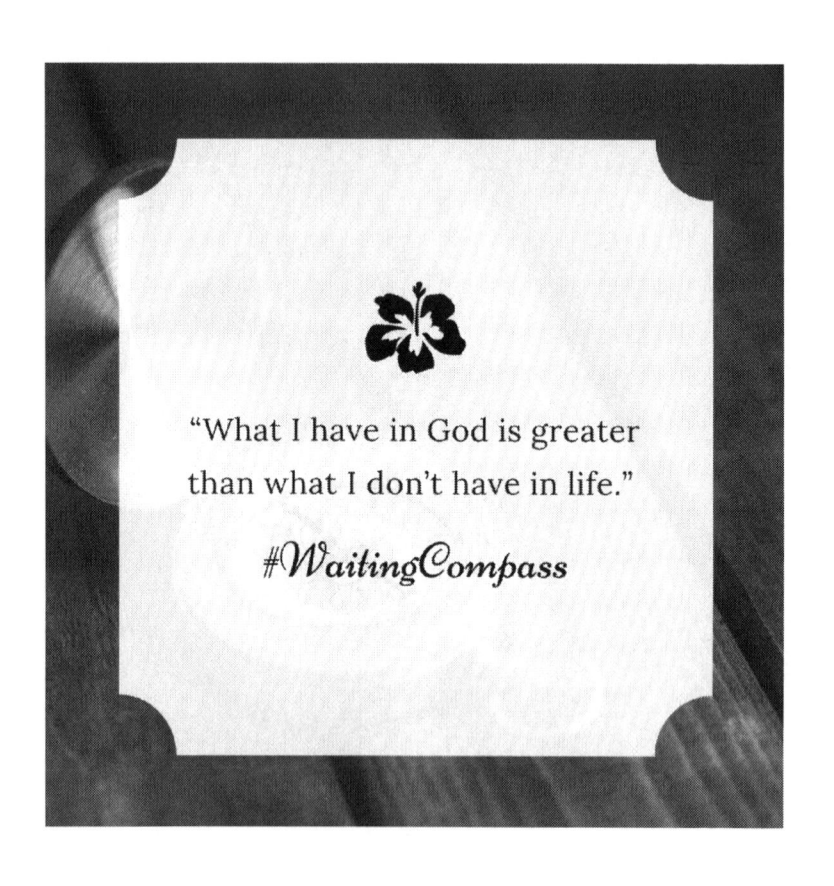

"What I have in God is greater than what I don't have in life."

#WaitingCompass

Question #1: How many copies of "you" did God make?

I branched at the white house the other day to do the two things I usually do there: to read and to feel convenient. (Guess you now know the "white house" I am referring to.) Within minutes, reading turned to surfing and surfing turned to Facebooking. No sooner had I switched to the Facebook app than my eyes fell on a notification:

Friend X shared a new photo

I clicked. The photo had a caption:

It's Official! I'm Married! Enjoying the wonders of Dubai with my HoneyPie!

Normally, I will just click on "Like" and mindlessly scroll on, but not that day. I was stunned!

My God! Is that Friend X? He's changed so much since high school! See how sharp and clean he looks in that white suit... and here I am, same age with him and I'm still single. Oh my world! I can't believe He's honeymooning in Dubai. He was always so smart in school; he must be filthy rich now. And he's married too!... And ugh, is that 265 likes and 196 comments I see? Oh my gosh! No one even cares about my Facebook posts anymore. Church. Writing. Editing. No me-time. My life is so boring and pathetic!

The not-so-nice effervescence from the white closet I sat upon snapped me back to reality. I was in the rest room, but far from being at rest.

Do you know that feeling?

While the above scenario isn't totally true (I've edited the narrative to align with the message I intend to pass across), it is in fact a scenario many of us can relate with. You see the wedding anniversary family photo of a colleague who you graduated from the same university the same year. She got married the same year as you. Now, they are celebrating their fifth anniversary and the family of two has become a family of four as two gorgeous kids have been added to the family. Almost naturally, your mind initiates a comparative analysis and generates a report that is downloaded directly to the server of your heart. All of a sudden, being married for five years without a child of your own becomes magnified as a disaster. You remember that you are supposed to be a child of God and that makes the report even worse because God has not been good *to you.*

Really?

It is unfortunate that the immediacy, versatility and universality of the social media has awakened humanity into a new normalcy where we have more and more *impressions* to compare ourselves and our accomplishments with—and thus, we have more and more reasons to have the joy snuffed out of our existence. No wonder more and more people are suffering from anxiety attacks on daily basis.

If the exit from the stage of *want* is to embrace contentment, then the first index of doing that is to nip comparison in the bud.

Don't get me wrong—contentment is not being passive or lazy—it's not the absence of ambition. Instead, contentment means that at every stage of your life, your happiness is measured by the acknowledgement of and gratitude for what you have, not postponed by dwelling on an inventory of what you are yet to get. And how do you make a habit of showing appreciation for what you have? You begin by resisting to compare yourself with others!

Ann Voskamp was right in saying that "Comparison is a thug that robs your joy. But it's even more than that—Comparison makes you a thug who beats down somebody—or your soul."[18]

> *She's married and I'm yet to find the right man.*
>
> *She's now a mother of two, yet I married earlier than her and I'm yet to have a child.*
>
> *We wrote the UTME CBT together but she had 230 while I was given 190—the same score I had last year!*

---

[18] "Ann Voskamp Quotes", *BrainyQuote* <https://www.brainyquote.com/quotes/ann_voskamp_628980>.

He's got 6 packs, I can't boast of 2.

He speaks so fluently; I stammer so annoyingly.

His face is so fresh; mine, so pimpled.

Can you allow me to bring you a few points to ponder?

For starters, know this: Scales always lie! That's not my idea, it's Ann Voskamp's. And beautifully, she writes:

> Scales always lie. They don't make a scale that ever told the truth about value, about worth, about significance.
>
> And the thing about measuring sticks, girl? Measuring sticks try to rank some people as big and some people as small—but we aren't sizes. We are souls. There are no better people or worse people—there are only God-made souls. There is no point trying to size people up, no point trying to compare—because souls defy measuring.
>
> You can't measure souls.
>
> And the moment you try to measure souls — you try to usurp God. And ain't nobody needs reminding of who it was that tried to usurp God. Measuring people is always devilish work—and carrying around a measuring stick is a bit like

carrying around a pitchfork.[19]

No man-made scale ever tells the truth about your worth. Remember, what you have in God is much more than what you lack in life. There is no point trying to size people up, no point trying to compare—because souls defy measuring. And when we compare, we're essentially telling God that what He created wasn't good enough.

> The world isn't a forest of measuring sticks. The world is a forest of burning bushes. Everything isn't a marker to make you feel behind or ahead; everything is a flame to make you see GOD is here.
>
> That God is working through this person's life, that God is redeeming that person's life, that God is igniting this work, that God is present here in this mess, that God is using even this.[20]

Paul was correct. He said concerning humans, "Certainly, when they measure themselves by themselves and compare themselves to themselves, they show how foolish they are"[21] Simple truth!

This makes even more sense when we come to terms with our individual uniqueness. How many copies of "you" did God make? The Psalmist responds, "He fashions (our) hearts **individually**."[22]

---

[19] Ann Voskamp, "How The Hidden Dangers Of Comparison Are Killing Us ... (And Our Daughters): The Measuring Stick Principle", *Huffpost*, 2014 <https://www.huffingtonpost.com/ann-voskamp/how-the-hidden-dangers-of_b_4232320.html?guccounter=1>.
[20] *Ibid.*
[21] 2 Corinthians 10:12 GW
[22] Psalm 33:15 NKJV

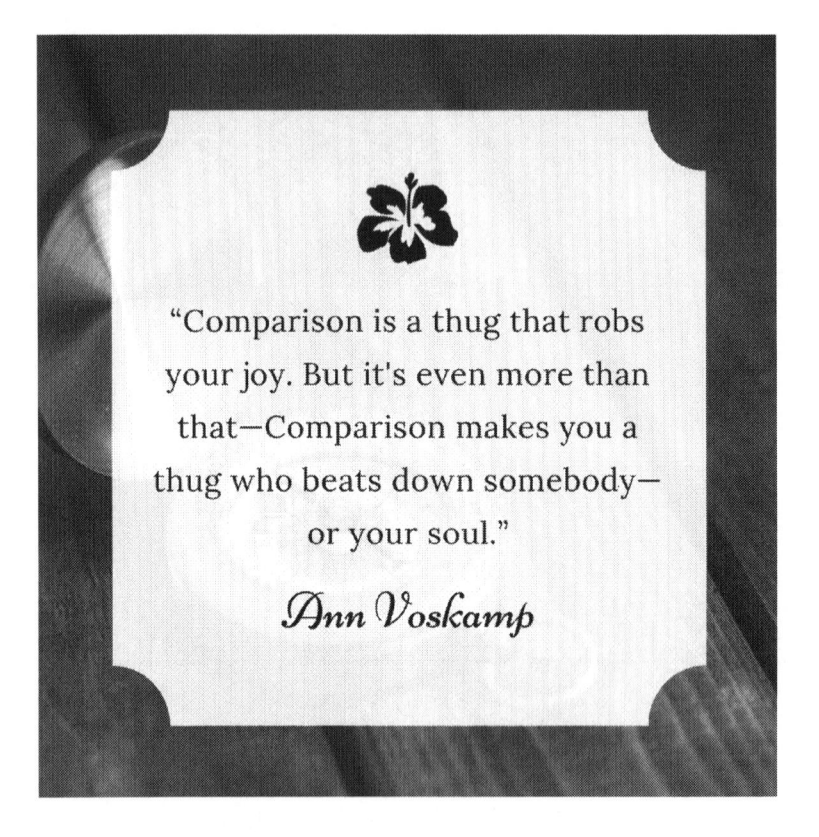

"Comparison is a thug that robs your joy. But it's even more than that—Comparison makes you a thug who beats down somebody— or your soul."

Ann Voskamp

Paul also says that we are God's workmanship—God's masterpiece—created in Christ Jesus to do good works.[23] My wife recently caught a revelation on that description of our identity quite recently and it radically changed how she started viewing herself and everyone else. "An artist would have many works on display", she said in a vlog to our mentees, "but the masterpiece will be his best work(s) and will naturally demand special display and extra protection." But in God's case, as the Ultimate Artist, He's got loads of works in His gallery, but every single one of those is a masterpiece in its own right!

As a poet, I also found it interesting that our English word "poem" comes from this Greek word translated "masterpiece" or "workmanship." You are not only a one-of-a-kind hand-crafted work of art made by God, you are also God's poem. You are not an assembly-line product, mass-produced without thought. You weren't an accident. You are a custom designed, one-of-a kind, original masterpiece. God carefully and painstakingly mixed the DNA cocktail that created you. You are wonderfully complex. You are one in a zillion! You might have been the product of a failed contraceptive, but essentially, God planned for you, configured you with special gifts and strategically located you in His world.

Such an incredible personal attention to detail with which God designed each of us caused David to burst into praise:

---

[23] See Ephesians 2:10

"I thank you, God, for making me so mysteriously complex! Everything you do is marvelously breathtaking. It simply amazes me to think about it! How thoroughly you know me, Lord!"
(Psalm 139:14 TPT)

By knowing that there are 60,000 varieties of beetles, we learn God likes variety. And because God loves variety, He wants us to be special. No single gift is given to everyone. Also, no individual receives all the gifts. If you had them all, you'd have no need of anyone else, and that would defeat one of God's purposes—to teach us to depend on each other.

Sweetheart, God doesn't make junk! You are beautiful as you are! After all, beauty is not from the eye of the beholder but from the hands of the Creator, and your Creator is the very best there is.

Check yourself out in the mirror and remind yourself, "I am the only me that God designed. He didn't make me accidentally, and He didn't form me with some societal standard in mind that He was trying to measure up to. He is infinitely creative and brilliant!"

Every time God creates, He does so with intention. He utilized an equal and exact amount of creativity when He made you, and every other person on this planet. When we choose to compare ourselves with others around us, or versions of themselves that people project on social media, we aren't only making life harder on ourselves, we are telling God He didn't do a good enough job.

The flaws you see in your body, or in your personality, or in your ability—they are not flaws to God. They are all to his glory! (Remember Track 1?) So if we continually compare ourselves to the people around us, we miss the opportunity to build others up and bring glory to God in what we can do right at this moment. Therefore, comparison is at its core selfish and prideful because it takes the focus off God and others and keeps it on ourselves.

You desire a way out of the comparison trap? Then learn to admire without having to acquire. Kelly Givens, the editor of iBelieve.com passed on a piece of counsel from a mentor: "Whenever you find you are comparing yourself to someone else, you should go right up to that person and compliment them on the very thing you're jealous of or comparing yourself to."[24] Jealous of someone's change of marital status? Congratulate him/her heartily! Jealous of someone's new bump? Offer to be a godparent to the unborn child. When our comparison points metamorphose into celebration points, the devil loses and God is glorified.

As you are waiting on God for that which you are trusting Him for, don't trust in displeasure; trust in satisfaction. Didn't we say that trust goes beyond believing that God can and beyond knowing that He is willing—it reaches to the even-if-He-doesn't threshold.

---

[24] Kelly Givens, "The Hidden Dangers of Comparison", *Crosswalk*, 2013 <https://www.crosswalk.com/blogs/christian-trends/the-hidden-dangers-of-comparison.html>.

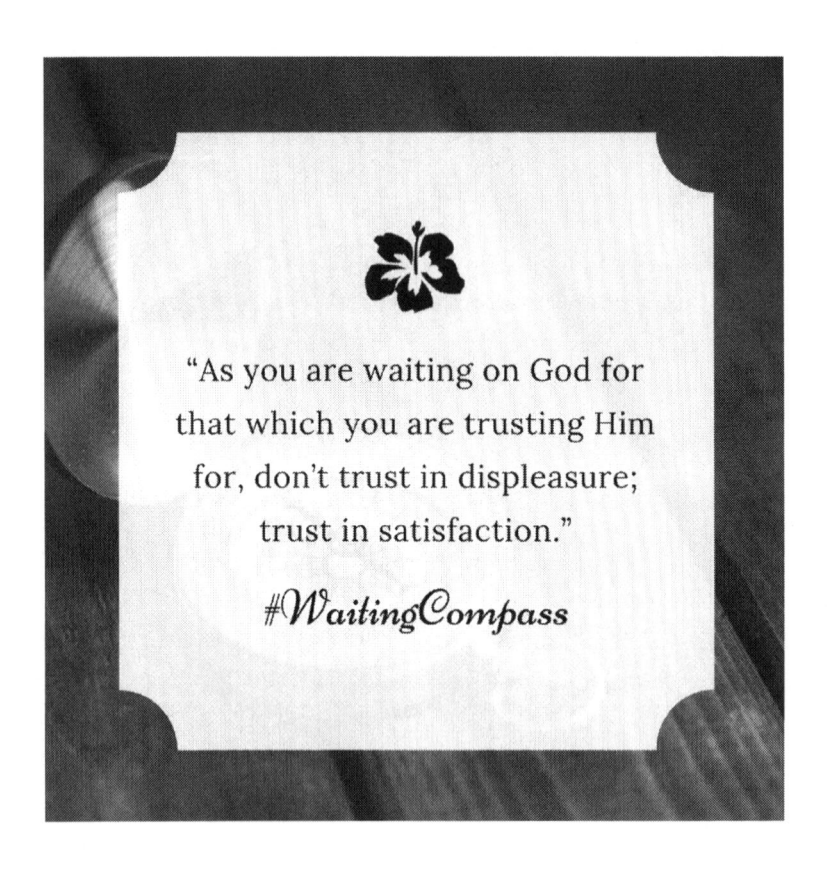

"As you are waiting on God for that which you are trusting Him for, don't trust in displeasure; trust in satisfaction."

#WaitingCompass

So what has been your point of comparison? Mine was the marital status, honeymoon experience and the geographical location of those newlyweds. It ate me up for a brief moment, but afterwards, the Holy Spirit ministered to me. If you forget any verse on the folly of discontent which manifests in comparisons, remember that "It's healthy to be content, but envy can eat you up."[25]

May you be preserved from such danger. Amen.

Question #2: Why would God ever bless you with what you are waiting on Him for?

It has been a tiring ride from Egbeda to Cement bus stop, no thanks to the heavy traffic. But it got worse before it got better. The bus was grossly inconvenient, the conductor was disturbingly vocal and the driver was obviously having a terrible day. We (the passengers) had no idea what was coming.

In the stand-still traffic jam, the driver opted to save some fuel by turning off the engine. No sooner had he done this than the traffic melted and started flowing. The driver tried to start the engine again but the engine refused to start. The driver rushed to a nearby filling station to buy some fuel. The conductor disappeared and reappeared with a keg of water. The engine took both but refused to start. The passengers, convinced that they've had enough, began a chorus:

"Refund our money, let's board another bus."

That was the chorus that rented the air. The troubled duo of the driver and conductor tried their

---

[25] Proverbs 14:30 CEV

best to calm the already frustrated passengers but couldn't do it. Reluctantly, the conductor returned each passenger's money. I got a nudge in my heart to take a look at the driver's face. I did, and compassion filled my heart.

I saw a man in despair. I saw a man asking in the loud whispers of his soliloquy "God, are You still there? Are you seeing this?" I saw a hungry wife, school drop-out children, and a hopeless husband. I saw everything but faith, hope and love... Compassion filled my heart!

While the other passengers were collecting their transport fares back from the conductor, I walked up to the driver and handed him the 2,000 naira I had on me apart from the other money I'd budgeted for my transportation and feeding for the day. That 2,000 naira was, at the time, my last kobo. My bank accounts were at their minimum balance, yet I told the driver, "add this to what you need to fix the bus." He was too shocked to show some gratitude. I was too quick to have noticed, even if he did. He watched me leave and join another bus, his mouth left agape.

****

I sat next to a teenage girl. She sat next to her dad. She was in the boarding house but her dad went to pick her from the school so that she could go and do her GCE registration. She was in her penultimate year in Grammar School. She never stopped talking with her dad—partly from the excitement of being with him again after quite a while, and partly from the knowledge she's acquired in school which she couldn't keep to herself.

She told her dad of her plans to put to practice the biogas production she learnt in school by turning their household waste to cooking gas… Her dad listened with pleasure. He wore a broad and obvious that's-my-girl smile. And once in a while, I couldn't help but chuckle at her remarks.

After an hour on the road, I knew intuitively that I'm sitting beside her for a purpose. The purpose wasn't clear yet until I started a conversation with her. She's very bright! She maintained an intelligent discussion with me, albeit reluctantly. But after a while, we flowed like pals. Her dad was pleased, too, I could tell.

Then all of a sudden, my purpose of sitting next to her became clear. "Pay for her GCE form", I perceived an inner voice say to me. Now, that was a very bad time for me to *squander* the little resources I had on a *perception*. What I had at that moment financially couldn't meet up the expenses I had on ground, yet, there was I with a pay-for-her-GCE-form voice ringing in my heart.

I swallowed a lump and asked her,

"Have you obtained your GCE form yet?"

"No", she replied.

"And do you know how much it is?"

"Not yet. I'll find out when my dad and I get to the registration centre"

In my estimation, the maximum amount I

thought a GCE form could cost was 5,000 naira. I didn't know that my estimation was a decade backwards. I made a couple of calls to find out the average price for the form. 13,500 naira. My heart froze!

In my bag was an envelope with 14,000 naira which was a much-awaited loan refund from a colleague upon which I'd placed my budget for that period. But in obedience, I took 500 naira from the envelope before sealing it.

"What's your name, my dear?"

"Rasheedat"

My heart froze again. I'm wasting 13,500 naira on a Muslim?

God thought otherwise! Your gifts are never a waste, they are eternal investments! King Solomon, reputed to be the wisest man to ever live, says

> *"There is one who scatters, and yet increases all the more, And there is one who withholds what is justly due, and yet it results only in want."*
> *(Proverbs 11:24 KJV)*

With a trembling hand, I wrote her name on the envelope and presented it to her. "That's for your GCE registration". She was stunned. She left my hand hanging in the presentation posture as she tapped her dad to let him into what was happening.

The rest, they say, is history!

****

I could go on and on to share stories after stories of how I'd resisted the urge to hoard and heeded the nudge to give. What a joy always follows! Unfortunately, this is a joy many people have not known.

When Hurricane Michael hit Florida in October 2018, various clips flooded the internet of whole houses floating on water and lots of people's belongings destroyed in the flood. It became apparent how pointless it is to hoard stuff. With all their belongings destroyed, these people are going to move on, and continue living.

At the end of the day, those perished stuff are merely just that…stuff. We call them *belongings* but in actual fact, they do not even belong to us. The Gospel of Mark tells the story of a poor widow who came to the temple and dropped in two small coins as an offering. She was down to her last pennies, yet rather than spend them on bread, she returned them to God. Financial gurus would have urged her to cut back on her giving. They would have discouraged the generosity of the woman. But Jesus did just the opposite. He said, "I tell you the truth, this poor widow has given more than all the others who are making contributions."[26] Jesus' point is clear: God owns everything—we are only stewards of what we have.

---

[26] Mark 12:43 KJV

"Jesus' point is clear: God owns everything—we are only **stewards** of what we *have*."

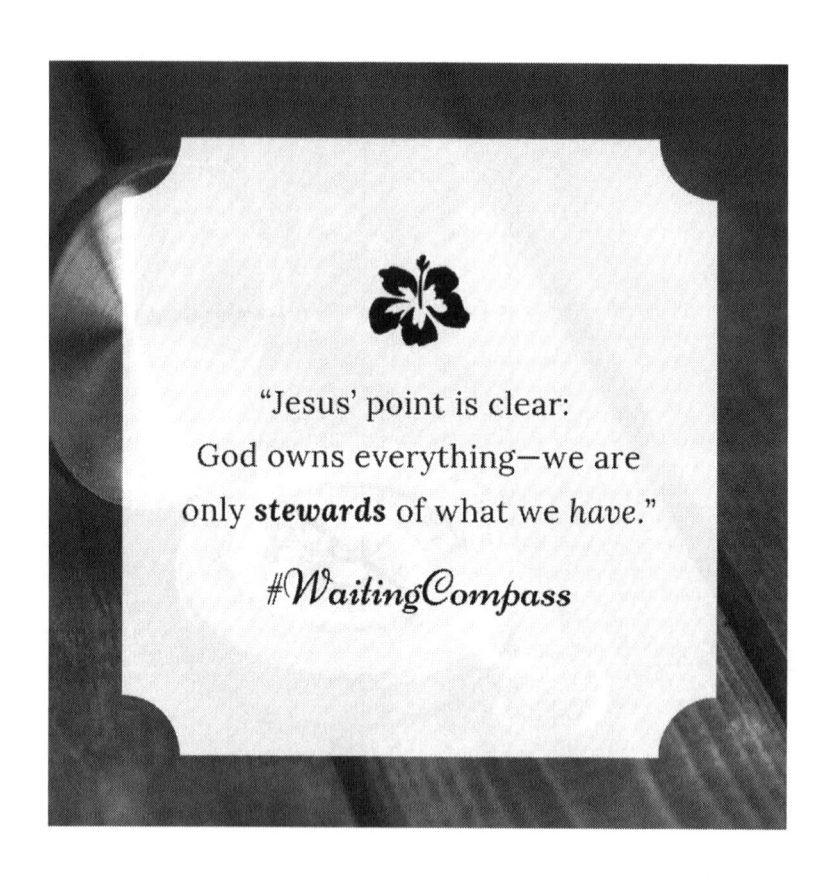

#*WaitingCompass*

Those who hoard rather than share had embraced three failures. They have failed to recognize God's Provision (Everything we have is because God provided it), failed to realize God's purpose (God's purpose for blessing us is so that we can be a blessing to others, too), and failed to regard God's plan (God's plan is that you will be comforted in comforting others, blessed in blessing others and favoured in favouring others).

How great the joy that comes from giving! While I never heard from the driver again, I couldn't forget his look of amazement in a hurry. And Rasheedat? I heard from her again. I did not notice that my colleague had put my name and mobile number on a corner of the envelope with which he packaged the refund. Rasheedat guessed it might be my number, and she guessed right. She called me to say thank you and she made me speak to all her family members. How soothing that was!

When you are waiting on God for one thing or the other, it is not a time to be passive in generosity; when your life models the understanding that whatever we receive from God is such that makes us channels of blessing to others, God can trust you with anything. It was the Shunamite woman's secret sauce. She started by showing hospitality to Elisha the prophet, then she gave him a room. Nine months later, she had become a mother—something she had desired for God knows how long.

I believe it's high time we moved from the fear of scarcity to the comfort of provision. Let's purposefully experience less hoarding and more sharing. Let's replace the fear of the coming winter with faith in the living God! Paul admonished us to do good, be rich in good works, ready to give, willing to share.[27]

May that be you!

Question #3: What do you have?

"What do I have?" is perhaps the question I have asked myself the most. I've asked it in various phrasings and I've given different answers. Looking back, though, there is an interesting trend in my responses…

(age 1)

Q: "What do I have in order to cater for my feeding expenses?"

A: "I have lovely parents"

(age 5)

Q: "What do I have in order to pay my school fees?"

A: "I have lovely parents"

(age 10)

Q: "What do I have in order to throw a 10th year birthday party?"

A: "Dad and Mum will take care of that"

(age 11)

Q: "What do I have in order to maintain my 5 year

---

[27] See 1 Timothy 6:17

unbroken record of topping my class?"

A: "Wake up earlier to read more and remind people that I am the best student"

(That term, I was beaten to second place by 2 points)

(age 16)
Q: "What do I have in order to facilitate an end to my negative addictions?"

A: "Make a new year resolution"

(The resolution was broken on the 2nd of January)

(age 17)
Q: "What do I have as a guarantee for an 'A' grade in MCB 202?"

A: "Divine guidance in my preparation"

(I had an unbelievable 'A' in the course)

(age 25)
Q: "What do I have in order to foot my bills if I give Rasheedat my last 13,500 to buy her GCE form?"

A: "I have Jehovah Jireh—God the Provider—on my side!"

(That night, I got a credit alert for 4 times the amount I gave Rasheedat)

The same question comes to each of us. How do we answer it?

****

We have examined the development of contentment through the lens of resisting the lure to make comparisons and releasing what we have to help others. Now, we turn to another important tool: rejoicing in what we have, now. Rather than getting depressed in the seeming delay of God to answer a particular prayer point, there is a surge of hope that comes from rejoicing in that which we have at the moment. Keep in mind the working principle of contentment: What I have in God is much more than what I lack in life.

The devil wants to magnify the one thing you do not have yet out of proportion till it overshadows the numerous other things that you have at the moment. Yes, you have something! And the simple truth is that none of us would have anything if it were not for the goodness of God. He wants us to enjoy what He has given to us. The Preacher says "It's better to enjoy what we have than to always want something else, because that makes no more sense than chasing the wind."[28] The same Preacher pointed out that "it is a good thing to receive wealth from God and the good health to enjoy it. To enjoy your work and accept your lot in life — that is indeed a gift from God."[29]

True happiness is definitely not in getting whatever you want; it is in enjoying whatever you have. Rather than hoping that a change in circumstances will bring a change in your attitude,

---

[28] Ecclesiastes 6:9 CEV
[29] Ecclesiastes 5:19 NLT

"The devil wants to magnify the one thing you do not have yet out of proportion till it overshadows the numerous other things that you have at the moment."

#WaitingCompass

embrace the blessed reminder that what you have in God at this very moment is greater than what you don't have in life.

Joni Eareckson Tada had been a quadriplegic for five decades. For 50 years, she had been on a wheel chair. She was not born like that. She knew what it felt like to run and to walk. She had full use of her leg until a diving accident at seventeen turned her into a quadriplegic. But she kept her faith and hope alive. The story of the man at the pool of Bethesda in John 5 became her favourite passage in all of scripture. This man had been an invalid for 38 years and even Jesus noted that 38 years was a long time to be in that condition.

> *"When Jesus saw him lying there, he knew that the man had been crippled for a long time. So Jesus said to him, "Do you truly long to be healed?""*
> *(John 5:6 TPT)*

Did you notice that Jesus' compassion, as John narrates, seems to be tied to the fact that this man had been crippled for a long time? So if 38 years was a long time, how about 40? 46? 50? Joni attended different healing crusades including a memorable crusade where Kathryn Kuhlman ministered. If there was a healing evangelist in America that could minister healing at the time, it would be Kathryn. So Joni attended the event, full of faith. But while there were healings in different parts of the room, the section where Joni sat amongst other wheel chair-bound folks seemed forgotten at the event. According to Joni,

> Before the service ended, ushers came to escort us all out of the wheel-chair section and to the elevators so as to not clog the hallways. And I could hear the organ music on the other side of the wall still playing as I sat, number 15 in a line of 35 disabled people at the elevator. We were all very quiet. And I looked up and down that line and I thought to myself, "Something is wrong with this picture. What kind of Savior? What kind of rescuer, what kind of healer, what kind of deliverer would refuse the prayer of a paralytic?[30]

Her disappointment in God drove her further away into loneliness and depression, but even there, God's comfort still descends usually as hymns. Until one day when she decides to pray,

> I cried out to God, "If I…If I can't live this way, then somebody else is going to have to. Jesus, You're going to have to do it for me. I can't do this thing called quadriplegia. Please show me how to live."[31]

Not long afterwards, she got back into the scriptures and hardly had she flipped open the Gospel according to Mark when her eyes were opened to this beautiful insight:

---

[30] "A Deeper Healing (Joni Eareckson Tada)", *Grace to You*, 2013 <https://www.gty.org/library/sermons-library/TM13-2/a-deeper-healing-joni-eareckson-tada>.
[31] Ibid.

I found out in the first chapter of the gospel of Mark…There Jesus is healing a great deal of diseased and disabled people all throughout the day and long past sunset. Next morning the crowds return, Simon and his companions go rushing looking for Jesus, but He's nowhere to be found. That's because Jesus had gotten up early and gone off to a solitary place…to pray. And when they finally find Him, they tell Him about this crowd of disabled and diseased people at the bottom of the hill all looking for healing. And I thought what Jesus responded to them was so curious because it says in the 38th verse, "Jesus said, **'Let's go somewhere else, to the nearby villages in towns where I can preach there because this is why I have come.'**" And that's when it hit me, O did it hit me. It's not that Jesus did not care about all those sick and diseased people, it's just their problems weren't His main focus. The gospel was. The gospel that says sin kills, hell is real, but God is merciful and His Kingdom can change you and Jesus is the way. And whenever people miss this, whenever they just started coming to Jesus to get their pain and problems fixed, the Savior would always back away. No wonder I had been so depressed. O my goodness. I was in to Jesus just to get my problems and my paralysis fixed. Yes, Jesus cares about suffering people. He cares when you've been paralyzed for 38 years, or 46 years… But the gospel of Mark showed me His priorities because the same man that healed blind eyes and withered hands is the same one who said, "Gouge out that eye, cut off that hand if it leads you into sin." I got the picture. To me, physical healing had always been the big deal, but to God, my soul was a much bigger deal…[32]

No wonder while Paul was chained and imprisoned in a Roman jail cell, he could still pen these beautiful command to the believers in Philippi,

> *"Be cheerful with joyous celebration in every season of life. Let joy overflow, for you are united with the Anointed One!"*
> *(Philippians 4:4 TPT)*

Aren't you?

Yes, you are yet to have a child of 'your own' but that hasn't changed the fact that you are a child of God—and that's awesome news! Yes, you've prayed and the healing has not come through but the greatest healing that can ever happen to anyone is the healing of the soul, and you've got that the moment you became a child of God. You've got a Father that loves you more than you love yourself or your lover. How do I know that? Because, amongst other things, He's got the hair on your head counted! As much as you claim to love yourself or that special person in your life, I'm positive that you are yet to be so madly in love that you got the hair on their head counted. That's how detailed, thorough and involved God is in your life. What you think to be insignificant, it matters to Him. He's madly in love with you—and that's

---

[32] Ibid.

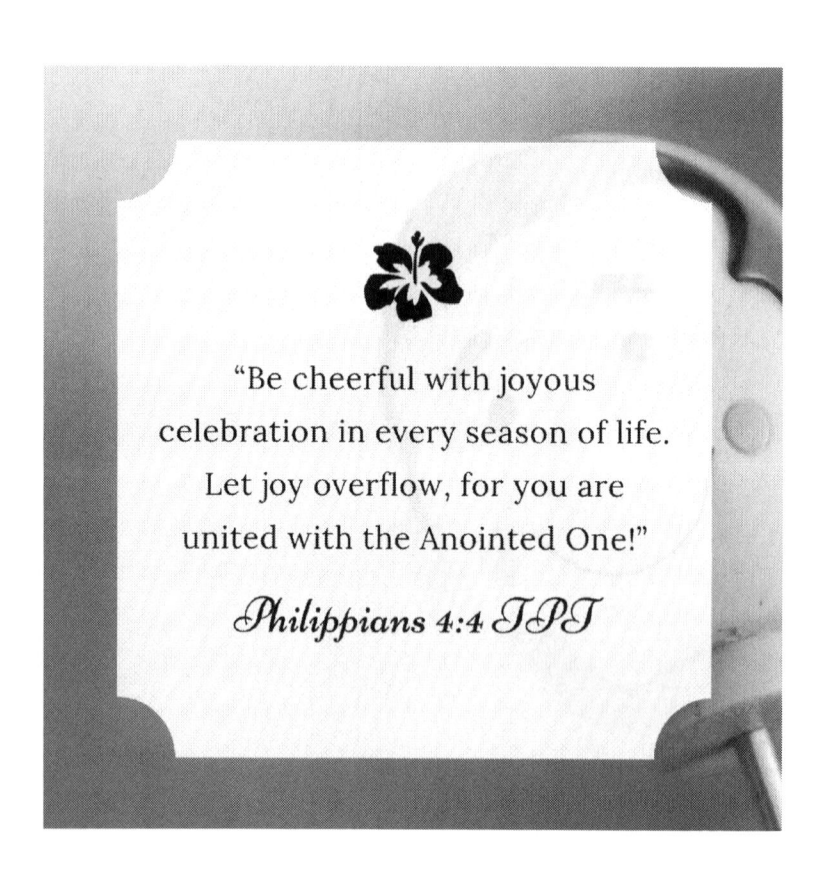

"Be cheerful with joyous celebration in every season of life. Let joy overflow, for you are united with the Anointed One!"

Philippians 4:4 TPT

something to not stop being grateful for.

When you look at life through the eyes of gratitude, the world becomes a wonderful place. Gratitude, as more and more experts have demonstrated, is probably the single most helpful attitude we can cultivate in seeking happier and healthier lives. And if a recent picture quote I saw on Facebook is worth anything, it's worth a ponder. It reads,

> *"If all you have today were the things you thanked God for yesterday, how much will you have?"*

Are you grateful for the *much more* that you have in God as opposed to what you lack in life? Are you even aware of the inexhaustible riches that you have in God? Before you are blinded by the needs and lacks of your life, embrace the blessed reminder that You have a Dad—your heavenly Father—Who hears you, you have the power of love behind you, the Holy Spirit within you, and all of heaven ahead of you. If you have Jesus, then "you have grace for every sin, direction for every turn, a candle for every corner, and an anchor for every storm. You have everything you need."[33]

And who can take it from you? Can economic breakdown affect the *daddyness* of God in your life? Can leukemia infect your salvation? Can bankruptcy impoverish your prayers? Hurricane Michael might take your earthly house, but will it touch your

---

[33] Traveling Light, p.32

heavenly home? I don't think so, too. No wonder the psalmist testified, "Then I pray to you, O Lord. I say, "You are my place of refuge. You are all I really want in life.""[34]

May that be your testimony, too.

Question #4: What are you living for?
March 2012,
Ile-Ife, State of Osun, Nigeria.

At about 2pm that afternoon, I was on my way to my bank. I alighted at Lagere from a commercial vehicle and crossed the road. As I was about to make a left, a young man caught up with me, panting.

"Are you Joseph Kolawole Ola?", he asked with high optimism plastered upon his face.

"Yes, I am. Pleased to meet you."

He screamed in ecstasy, then he hugged me. He couldn't contain himself.

"Wow! Are you serious? You look a little younger than your profile picture. Oh, pardon my manners—I'm one of your friends on Facebook. I follow every of your notes and I'm blessed by each piece. Your status updates, too have been a blessing. I'm glad to finally meet you!"

I smiled. He was so excited that he forgot to tell me his name. And I was so shocked, I couldn't ask. If I see him today, I'm positive I can't recognise him. By the time we parted ways, I was left with one question: "What's special about the notes and status updates,

---

[34] Psalm 142:5 NLT

anyways?"

****

June 2013,
Idimu/Ikotun Road, Lagos State, Nigeria.

I was transferred from my former station to an assembly in Ilesa, State of Osun in May 2013 as a Student Pastor. I was posted back to Lagos on the 1st of June, same year. My three weeks at Ilesa was quite eventful and memorable, but the story I'm reliving in the next few lines happened on my return to Lagos. It is an experience I will never forget in a hurry.

Shortly after my return to Lagos, I visited the filling station closest to my church. I was a regular customer there before my transfer to Ilesa. The transfer came rather suddenly so I didn't get to bid the filling station attendants farewell. Three weeks had passed and they had not seen me. Then one of them spotted me from afar.

She screamed so loud, all their customers thought something was wrong. They traced the direction of her excited gaze…and there I was. Before you could say "Jack", the other attendants joined in the scream.

"Pastor! Our very own pastor!"

"But pastor you no try o. How you go commot like that, you no fit tell person"

"Pastor, what did you bring for us"

"Pastor, are you finally back, or you are going again?"

They were all talking simultaneously. I was shocked and embarrassed. You would have thought it was an *Area Father* that stepped into the midst of some *Area Boys*. I was really embarrassed.

They fought over who will dispense the fuel I came to buy. I got a more-than-executive treatment at their station. Me? The odd thing about the story is that I did not even have a car. Most of the time, I come to the filling station with kegs to buy fuel for my church's generator. Yet, I felt like their biggest customer.

As I headed back to church, I was asking myself... "What have I done to deserve this royal welcome-back from, well, from folks you may never find in church?" The Holy Spirit stopped me in my track and reminded me: "Jesus—your chief example—also earned Himself the title "A Friend of Sinners."

Like Jesus, like me; like Father, like son!

****

Don't forget where we started from in this discourse on contentment. We asked ourselves, What is the one thing separating you from joy? When will you be truly happy? When you are healed? Or promoted? Or married? Or become pregnant? Or rich? Then we took it further: What if the situation never changes? What if your dream never comes true? Could you be happy?

I believe the answer is yes! Hence Jesus' counsel,

> *"Don't be greedy for what you don't have. Real life is not measured by how much we own."*
> *(Luke 12:15 NLT)*

In other words, true happiness is not gotten from materialism; true happiness is gotten from experiencing and expressing your reason for living. True happiness comes from prioritizing souls and investing in them. True happiness comes from refocusing on what is going to last. The bible word for it is *godliness*. Godliness focuses our attention on eternity. Godliness reminds us that we shall be accountable to God on the last day. Godliness reminds us that everything earthly is temporary. Godliness urges us to give our attention to permanent values and reorganize our lives around eternal priorities. Ultimate gain in life is like Twin Towers, the name of one is godliness, and the other is contentment.

> *But godliness with contentment is great gain.*
> *(1 Timothy 6:6 NIV)*

> *For we fix our attention, not on things that are seen, but on things that are unseen. What can be seen lasts only for a time; but what cannot be seen lasts forever.*
> *(2 Corinthians 4:18 GNT)*

Materialism clouds our vision of God, and we begin to think that all there really is to life is getting

"Happiness is not all about getting what you want... True happiness is gotten from **experiencing and expressing your reason for living**; from **prioritising souls** and **investing in them**; from **refocusing on what is going to last**."

#WaitingCompass

and enjoying things. As such, our perspective gets warped. Which begs the concluding question in this discourse: What are you living for? How would you want to be remembered a century away? Or, better question, how would you want to be rewarded in eternity?

> On this side of eternity, the truth remains that the vast majority of us won't win a gold medal...and that's okay! We understand in the economy of earth there are a limited number of crowns. The economy of heaven, however, is refreshingly different! Heavenly rewards are not limited to a chosen few, but "to all those who have longed for his appearing" (2 Timothy 4:8). The 3 letter word "ALL" is a gem. In heaven, the winner's circle isn't reserved for a handful of the elite, but for a heaven full of God's children that "will receive the crown of life that God promised to those who love Him" (James 1:12)...For all we don't know about the next life, this much is certain. The day Christ comes will be a day of reward. Those who went unknown on earth will be known in heaven.[35]

Indeed imagine what that will look like. It is glorious beyond description. That is where our focus should be. The more you keep eternity in perspective, the less unhappy you find your waiting season and the more blissful living becomes. Your waiting itself will begin to shift from waiting for things to waiting for Him. And if there is anything we can be sure of, He

---

[35] Max Lucado, *When Christ Comes* (Nashville, Tennessee: Thomas Nelson, 2014), pp. 70-71.

will come again!

So God delays and keeps us waiting.
Not in scorn, but in wisdom, unfailing
He isn't idle when He doesn't answer;
Neither is He wicked when He doesn't waver

#WaitingCompass

The God of Happy Endings

I remember an incident that happened on the 4th of August 2015 few days after I launched Alive Mentorship Group. On that day, I forgot my wallet in a public bus and shared a lesson or two about the experience with the members of the mentoring group. Thanks to WhatsApp chat export function, I still have a record of my exact words which was posted at 10:22pm (Nigerian Time).

    Good evening, family. Trust our days went well.

    I'm just getting back home after a very long day at my church's ongoing annual international convention and thought to share with you an experience I had about 30 minutes ago.

I forgot my wallet in a public bus.

As I alighted from the bus at Council Bus Stop (my final stop), I discovered almost immediately after the bus zoomed off... So, I boarded another bus as quickly as I could to trace the bus in which I forgot the wallet. The final stop for all the buses that ply that route is Ikotun BRT Bus Stop—a very busy bus stop at that time of the night.

I got there and tried to locate the bus in which I'd forgotten the wallet but there were so many buses, all looking alike and I couldn't locate the recognizable face of the bus conductor.

I didn't find the wallet.

I don't have much cash in it but some really important valuables including all my ATM cards, my voter's card and my expired driver's license amongst few other business cards and passport photographs. I came back home, however, UNPERTURBED.

...and that's why I'm sharing this...

I'm aware that as you keep doing life, you will find out that life brings us surprises sometimes, some pleasant and some others unpleasant, but there's a realm of living in which, irrespective of what is going on, you will be at peace.

I feel like that's what I'm experiencing right now.

Trust me, I'm not saying this to psyche anybody up; it's the truth. I misplaced my wallet, yes. But am I disturbed about it? No.

Here are few reasons why I'm not disturbed:

1. There's no use crying over spilt milk.

2. I did try my best to find it...

3. I refuse to link the occurrence to whatever I might have done wrong earlier in the day as the devil would want me to (and, no, I haven't been perfect all day). Instead, I choose to live in the reality of the 'no condemnation' promise of God's Word to those who are saved.

4. (and most importantly), I've left it in the hands of him that cares for me. (1 Peter 5:7).

Will He make me find it again in some miraculous way? I know He can, but I can't say for certain if He will. But this much, I know:

WHENEVER YOU LEAVE A MATTER IN HIS HANDS, YOU CAN GO TO SLEEP.

And that's exactly what I'm going to do.

Love you loads.

Good night.

That was 10:22pm. Would you believe it if I told you that twenty minutes later, I was on my way to meeting the young man that found the wallet? Shortly after my 10:22pm post, I saw that a number I couldn't recognise started 'flashing' my line. I decided to call the number back and—simply following a leading I sensed in my spirit—record the conversation. It turned out to be the young man that found the wallet on the other end of the line. He boarded the bus just after I alighted from the bus but held on to the wallet not trusting that it will get to me if he handed it over to the bus conductor or driver. I dropped the recording of my conversation with the young man on my mentoring group and by 10:54pm, I posted on the group: "I have collected it."

These young folks were so excited. Many of them came online to rejoice and celebrate how God could promptly intervene when matters are left in his hand. Some of them even sent in voice notes of their songs of thanksgiving. It almost felt like a thanksgiving vigil on a WhatsApp group.

Indeed, we serve a God of happy endings and we are always ever-so-pleased to experience that side of Him. We rejoice when a missing wallet is found in the name of Jesus. We rejoice when the sickness is swallowed up instantly by the healing power of Jesus. We rejoice when the 'F' is miraculously turned into an 'A' because sister Betty prayed and fasted before going to see her course coordinator. We are uber-glad when the Christian couple that had been barren for two decades gives birth to a set of twins. We resonate with such movies as *Miracles from Heaven* when tragedy upon tragedy in a Christian family ends in such a happy ending. We love happy endings!

But what if the wallet was never found in spite of

casting my cares on Jesus? (By the way, the same wallet got lost again later that same week, and this time, I never found it again.) What if the sickness lingered? What if the 'F' remained an 'F' no matter what you did? What if those couple never gets to carry a child born from their union till the day of their death? What if Abby in *Miracles from Heaven* actually remained dead when she hit the bottom of the tree into which she fell? Does that change God's interest in giving His children happy endings?

I have learnt from at least 3 people how to answer that. One of them, we've read her story in the previous chapter—Joni Eareckson Tada; let's move on to the second; John 'the Baptist'.

He was Jesus' cousin. More than that, he was Jesus' forerunner. He knew more than anyone else that Jesus is the Messiah. When Jesus came by to be baptised by him in River Jordan, John was quick to announce to everyone there present, "Look! There he is—God's Lamb! He will take away the sins of the world!"[36] So if anyone knew who Jesus was, John did. But months later after the baptism, John was arrested. He had called out Herod's error in divorcing his wife to marry his brother's wife and Herod had him arrested and thrown into the dungeon. The bible is clear about how that story ended: John the Baptist was beheaded and his head was served on a platter to a ravenous enemy. It makes us wonder: "Is this how God repays those who have embraced the path of faithfulness? Is this how He celebrates those He has

---

[36] John 1:29 TPT

chosen? With imprisonment and a shameful death?"

Backing up a bit, however, between being arrested and being beheaded, there was an episode. The gospels recorded it thus: "John the Baptist, who was now in prison, heard about all the miracles the Messiah was doing, so he sent his disciples to ask Jesus, "Are you really the one we are waiting for, or shall we keep on looking?""[37] I think I would do the same. If you were the Messiah (which means 'saviour') why don't you start by saving me? Is a Messiah not supposed to defend the course of the righteous? Is the Saviour not supposed to show people whose side God is on by vindicating the helpless? But while John was imprisoned, Jesus was busy doing business as usual and practically acting unconcerned. Or so it seemed.

How did Jesus respond to the doubts of John? He replied, "Jesus told them, "Go back to John and tell him what you have heard and seen—the blind see, the lame walk, those with leprosy are cured, the deaf hear, the dead are raised to life, and the Good News is being preached to the poor.""[38] Summary? "Tell John, "everything is going as planned; the kingdom is being inaugurated!"" On this narrative, Max Lucado comments:

> John had been listening for an answer to his earthly problems, while Jesus was busy resolving his heavenly ones. That's worth remembering the next time you hear the silence of God. If you've asked

---

[37] Matthew 11:2-3 TLB
[38] Matthew 11:4-5 NLT

for a mate, but are still sleeping alone. . . if you've asked for a child, but your womb stays barren. . . if you've asked for healing, but are still hurting. . . don't think God isn't listening. He is. And he is answering requests you are not even making.[39]

If you have some Johns or Jonis in your world or you feel like you see them each time you look in a mirror, then take comfort. God is yet planning a happy ending for you. His silence doesn't mean that He cares less. He is busy at work setting you up for the most amazing happy ending. For all we know, besides the limitless joys and indescribable bliss that pervades the life to come when we get to see and be with the Lord forever, there is an icing on the cake for the likes of John and Joni. Revelations 2:10 describes a crown of life (a figurative expression of a special reward) for all those who endured some form of suffering or persecution for righteousness sake, whether that looks like John suffering for calling a spade a spade or like Joni for enduring the pains and limitations of living life in her circumstances.

This brings me to the third person that taught me how to answer the question of whether God still gives happy endings or not. His name is Greg Morse, a staff writer for desiringGod.org. Greg's little brother is autistic and he prayed to God every day to heal his little brother and free him from the captivity of autism. Eighteen years have gone, and that prayer is yet to be answered. But Greg believes, and so do I,

---

[39] Max Lucado, "Trusting More, Worrying Less - Max Lucado", *Max Lucado* <https://maxlucado.com/trusting-more-worrying-less/>.

that, it's only a matter of time. He writes,

> You and I are traveling—more quickly than it often seems—to the coming kingdom of *answered* prayer. To our Father's kingdom, which he has been pleased to give to his Son and other sons and daughters. We are but days from home. We may not remember all that we prayed for along the way, but God does, and rest assured, he will prove his faithfulness. He will show the unseen blessing of every well-disguised answer to prayer that, while squinting in this world, we only saw as unanswered. And his wisdom, as he peels back his dealings with us layer by layer, will satisfy our questions and arouse in us a love that unbelief tells us now cannot be. And we will sing what we could sometimes only stammer on earth: "He works *all things* for good for those who love him, who have been called according to his purposes" (see Romans 8:28). *All things* includes unanswered prayers. No prayer, like none of his lost sheep, will go unaccounted for or overlooked. For now, sore knees and aching backs cry, "I believe; help my unbelief!" (Mark 9:24). Soon enough death will end our prayer sessions, and we will wake to see our Lord face-to-face and find our prayers answered better than we could have asked.[40]

When I first shared these thoughts about a 'God of Happy Endings' with my mentees, one of them sent me a message that seemed apt to wrap up this

---

[40] Greg Morse, "For Every Prayer That Goes Unanswered", *Desiring God*, 2018 <https://www.desiringgod.org/articles/for-every-prayer-that-goes-unanswered>.

discourse.

> Good morning sir.
>
> I wanted to write to you to just pour out my heart about some things I was going through when I read your post this morning. But then...[t]he faithfulness of God being expounded in my heart by the Holy Ghost won't let me complain.
>
> So now I just want to say that God is faithful and really He's a God of happy endings...even though there are tragic interludes. And one thing my spiritual father always says is that when you're tired and about to give up, the devil is tired and about to give up as well. You determine who gives up first, you or the devil. I choose to keep on till the devil gives up. I'm not giving up at the edge of my breakthrough. God promised that the road will be possible, not necessarily easy. And just when the devil gives up again, I'm going to look the devil in the face and shout my victory! I'll tell him he lost again! I'll tell him Christ has won for me for all times! There might be tears in my eyes right now, but I have God's Word that my weeping will be turned to rejoicing, to dancing! The devil came too late and too little! Christ already won for me! And so, I'll keep waiting.

Need I say more? Indeed, He's a God of happy endings. Tragic interludes, yes; but an interlude announces that the music is not over. So, hang on! Keep waiting. This will end in joy.

I'll end this volume with a poem I wrote years back at the depth of the valley of my delay experience.

I've titled it "I WILL WAIT FOR HIM."

I Will Wait for Him

Once upon a tree of sin
Love did speak withholding nothing
But now beneath my valley's woe
The silence of Love is now my foe

Oh that Love may see the famine
And hasten the harvest—the kids are starving
Here are mothers praying for their fries
Oh that Love may hearken to their cries

But now I know in the summer and the cold
Trial and Love are brothers in the fold
Problem and time—born on the same day
And through our history, their thread has its way

Noah built his ark from the craziest instructions
The sun still shining in unclouded radiations
Abraham got his promise when time was past,
But years it took, though his faith was cast

David was dramatically chosen and anointed
Yet, on the hills, as a felon he was hounded
And Paul ministered with a thorn in his flesh
Waking daily in the dilemma of his mesh

From Love and Delays this lesson I've learnt
Faithful is He who feeds the ants
We share in the fellowship of all the saints,
By all our sufferings…and all our gains!

The great delays in the mystery of providence
Are chariots of goodies on the street of excellence
For the problems of yesterday are all but rocky—
A breath of tomorrow's wind, and all is memory.

Had I not wept all through the night
The morning joy would glow with lesser light
The same was true of Mary and Martha
Their dead was raised—a glory like no other

So God delays and keeps us waiting.
Not in scorn, but in wisdom, unfailing
He isn't idle when He doesn't answer;
Neither is He wicked when He doesn't waver

WAITING COMPASS

The sunshine of May lights up the world in green,
Yet in January's eyes, that vision was first seen
So when we pray and nothing happens,
In the heat of silence, our trust-sword sharpens

Speed is but one of the relative terms;
He makes all things beautiful on His own terms
There is more love in God's many 'power cuts'
Than our feigning wisdom; yes, our shortcuts

Starve your doubt and its devil
Stay with Love, He'll never stumble
He makes all things beautiful…
In His season—when it's best fruitful.

"I will wait for Him!"—this choice I make
Now unto you—what will be your take?

There is more love in God's many
power cuts
Than the feigning wisdom in
man's many shortcuts

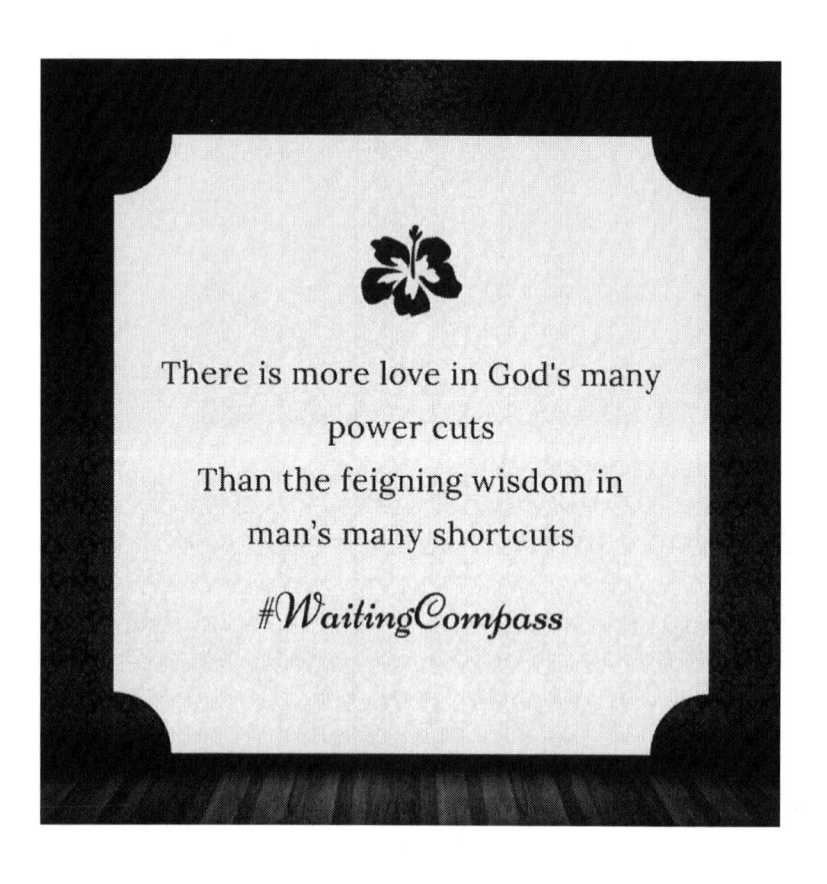

#WaitingCompass

References

"A Deeper Healing (Joni Eareckson Tada)", *Grace to You*, 2013 <https://www.gty.org/library/sermons-library/TM13-2/a-deeper-healing-joni-eareckson-tada>

"Ann Voskamp Quotes", *BrainyQuote* <https://www.brainyquote.com/quotes/ann_voskamp_628980>

Cole, Steven J., "Lesson 64: God's Delays (Acts 24:24-27)", *bible.org*, 2013 <https://bible.org/seriespage/lesson-64-god-s-delays-acts-2424-27>

"Derek Redmond finishes at the Olympics", *Stories for Preaching* <http://storiesforpreaching.com/derek-redmond-finishes-at-the-olympics/>

"Esther, Book of—New World Encyclopedia", *New World Encyclopedia*, 2017 <http://www.newworldencyclopedia.org/entry/Esther,_Book_of#Timeline_of_Major_Events>

Givens, Kelly, "The Hidden Dangers of Comparison", *Crosswalk*, 2013 <https://www.crosswalk.com/blogs/christian-trends/the-hidden-dangers-of-comparison.html>

Greear, J.D., "When You Can't Feel God", *Faithgateway*, 2015 <http://www.faithgateway.com/when-you-cant-feel-god>

Lucado, Max, "Trusting More, Worrying Less - Max Lucado", *Max Lucado* <https://maxlucado.com/trusting-more-worrying-less/>

Lucado, Max, *When Christ Comes* (Nashville, Tennessee: Thomas Nelson, 2014).

Meyer, Joyce, "How the Habit of Trust Transforms Your Life", *Joyce Meyer Ministries*, 2015 <https://www.joycemeyer.org/articles/ea.aspx?article=how_trusting_god_can_transform_your_life>

Meyer, Joyce, "When God's Timing Is Taking Too Long", *Joyce Meyer Ministries* <https://joycemeyer.org/everydayanswers/ea-teachings/when-gods-timing-is-taking-too-long>

Morse, Greg, "For Every Prayer That Goes Unanswered", *Desiring God*, 2018 <https://www.desiringgod.org/articles/for-every-prayer-that-goes-unanswered>

"Perseverance", *Sermon Illustrations*, 1989 <http://www.sermonillustrations.com/a-z/p/perseverance.htm>.

Stanley, Andy, *Irresistible* (Zondervan, 2018).

Voskamp, Ann, "How The Hidden Dangers of

Comparison Are Killing Us ... (And Our Daughters): The Measuring Stick Principle", *Huffpost*, 2014 <https://www.huffingtonpost.com/ann-voskamp/how-the-hidden-dangers-of_b_4232320.html?guccounter=1>

About The Book

This first instalment in the #Peaces Series explores the subject of GOD'S DELAYS. Time and again we have all been in scenarios where we (or someone we know) hoped that God will come through regarding one thing or the other but He didn't—at least, not when we were expecting Him to. It can be a frustrating place to be. But in five 'peaces' of helpful thoughts, Joseph points us in the direction where God may be found in times like that. The book was written with such simplicity and clarity that drives home the message and leaves the seeker immersed in the unwavering hope of God's reassuring promise: "I will never leave you, nor forsake you."

About The Author

Joseph is a young writer who is passionate about sharing the countercultural principles of the bible in easy-to-read works. He holds a Masters Degree in Biblical and Pastoral Theology from Liverpool Hope University, UK and a Pastoral Ministry certificate from Life Church College, Bradford.
He founded Alive Mentorship Group (AMG) in 2015— an online mentoring platform for teenagers and young adults with a growing outreach to over a thousand members in over twenty nations scattered across all the continents. Through AMG, Joseph and his wife are leveraging on social media's broad reach to pour into other young adults and teenagers practical life lessons from their daily experiences.
He pastors in The Apostolic Church from his base in Liverpool. He blogs at www.josephkolawole.org
He is blissfully married to Anu (http://eleosblisshouse.org) and together, they have a cute boy named Joshua.

Word Alive

Inspired by what you just read?
Connect with Joseph.

Word Alive.
Truth. Freedom. Growth.

Follow Joseph's teaching ministry, Word Alive, online. Visit www.JosephKolawole.org to get FREE resources for your spiritual growth and encouragement, including:

Blog Posts
Downloads of video, audio, and printed material
Joseph's podcast
First look at book excerpts
Mobile content.

You will also find an eStore and special offers.

www.JosephKolawole.org
+447752398481

Follow Joseph on Twitter @iamJosephOla
Or at Facebook.com/JosephKolawole

Printed in Poland
by Amazon Fulfillment
Poland Sp. z o.o., Wrocław